Bringing Innovative Practices to Your School

Exploring issues of student agency, equity, assessment, teaching, management, teacher leadership, and use of technology, this book provides strategies, tips, and guidance for enacting innovative change in today's schools. Drawing from unique and creative approaches at international schools, real practitioners share their stories and best practices. Chapters contain engaging snapshots of the innovative practices currently happening in international schools, translate those practices into leadership actions, and show how those innovations are played out in localized contexts. This exciting book is for every school and district leader keen to think outside the box, reassess their schools' strengths, and improve the purposes and means by which they educate students.

Jayson W. Richardson is an Associate Professor of Educational Leadership Studies at the University of Kentucky, and is a Director of the Center for the Advanced Study of Technology Leadership in Education (CASTLE).

Other Eye On Education Books Available from Routledge
(www.routledge.com/eyeoneducation)

Working with Students That Have Anxiety: Creative Connections and Practical Strategies
Beverley H. Johns, Donalyn Heise, and Adrienne D. Hunter

Implicit Bias in Schools: A Practitioner's Guide
Gina Laura Gullo, Kelly Capatosto, and Cheryl Staats

Five Practices for Improving the Success of Latino Students: A Guide for Secondary School Leaders
Christina Theokas, Mary L. González, Consuelo Manriquez, and Joseph F. Johnson Jr.

Leadership in America's Best Urban Schools
Joseph F. Johnson, Jr, Cynthia L. Uline, and Lynne G. Perez

Leading Learning for ELL Students: Strategies for Success
Catherine Beck and Heidi Pace

The Superintendent's Rulebook: A Guide to District Level Leadership
Patrick Darfler-Sweeney

The Hero Maker: How Superintendents Can Get Their School Boards to Do the Right Thing
Todd Whittaker

Bravo Principal!: Building Relationships with Actions That Value Others, 2nd Edition
Sandra Harris

Advocacy from A to Z
Robert Blackburn, Barbara R. Blackburn, and Ronald Williamson

20 Formative Assessment Strategies That Work: A Guide Across Content and Grade Levels
Kate Wolfe Maxlow and Karen L. Sanzo

7 Steps to Sharing Your School's Story on Social Media
Jason Kotch & Edward Cosentino

Rigor in Your School: A Toolkit for Leaders, 2nd Edition
Ronald Williamson and Barbara R. Blackburn

Lead with Me: A Principal's Guide to Teacher Leadership, 2nd Edition
Anita Pankake and Jesus Abrego, Jr.

Bringing Innovative Practices to Your School

Lessons from International Schools

Jayson W. Richardson

NEW YORK AND LONDON

First published 2020
by Routledge
52 Vanderbilt Avenue, New York, NY 10017

and by Routledge
2 Park Square, Milton Park, Abingdon, Oxon, OX14 4RN

Routledge is an imprint of the Taylor & Francis Group, an informa business

© 2020 Taylor & Francis

The right of Jayson W. Richardson to be identified as the author of the editorial material, and of the authors for their individual chapters, has been asserted in accordance with sections 77 and 78 of the Copyright, Designs and Patents Act 1988.

All rights reserved. No part of this book may be reprinted or reproduced or utilized in any form or by any electronic, mechanical, or other means, now known or hereafter invented, including photocopying and recording, or in any information storage or retrieval system, without permission in writing from the publishers.

Trademark notice: Product or corporate names may be trademarks or registered trademarks, and are used only for identification and explanation without intent to infringe.

Library of Congress Cataloging-in-Publication Data
A catalog record for this title has been requested

ISBN: 978-0-367-18589-3 (hbk)
ISBN: 978-0-367-18590-9 (pbk)
ISBN: 978-0-429-19706-2 (ebk)

Typeset in Optima
by Cenveo® Publisher Services

Contents

Introduction: Innovative Leadership Practices
in International Schools viii
Contributor Biographies xii

SECTION I: STUDENT AGENCY 1

1. *iBlock* @ UNIS Hanoi: Turning Potential into Performance 3
   Glenda Baker

2. Vignette: Classrooms Without Teachers 13
   Shwetangna Chakrabarty and Natasha Haque

3. Vignette: Innovate, Play, Transform: Design Thinking
   in the Early Years 16
   Kristen L. MacConnell

4. Vignette: Developing Creativity in Schools 19
   Sarah Ssengendo

SECTION II: EQUITY 23

5. A Journey to Inclusion 25
   Ryan Elissa Hopkins-Wilcox and Deborah Bradshaw

6. In Pursuit of International Mindedness 37
   Natasha Haque

7. Women in Science: Community Collaboration
   for Real-World Inquiry 48
   Stephanie Budd and Caleb Steindam

SECTION III: CURRICULUM, TEACHING, AND STUDENT LEARNING — 59

8. Skill-Based Exams: Assessment Promoting the Transfer of Learning Beyond the Classroom — 61
   Jim Gerhard and Gray Macklin

9. Creating Curriculum Structures That Foster Innovation — 71
   Elizabeth Rossini

10. Vignette: Personal Learning Profiles: Learning for the Unique, Not the Average — 81
    Daniel Todd

SECTION IV: MANAGEMENT OF SCHOOLS — 85

11. Instructional Coaches: An Investment in Innovation — 87
    Kimberly Ann Cofino

12. Bringing Innovative Practices to Traditional Contexts: Navigating the Challenges of Change — 98
    Jennifer D. Klein

13. The Future of Learning at the Western Academy of Beijing: A Work in Progress — 110
    John D'Arcy

14. A Reimagined Doctoral Program — 122
    Matthew Militello and Lynda Tredway

SECTION V: TEACHER LEADERSHIP — 133

15. Cultivating Teacher Leadership — 135
    Kristen L. MacConnell

16. Vignette: Distributed Leadership Through Reciprocal Advisory Structures — 146
    Joelle Basnight

17. Creating a Culture of Learning — 150
    Ryan Elissa Hopkins-Wilcox

18.	Visiting Scholars: Bring Innovation to You! Kimberly Ann Cofino	161
19.	A Reimagined Doctoral Program in Action: Confronting Equity Challenges in International Schools Matthew Militello, Lynda Tredway, Tosca Killoran, Christie Powell and Kristin Halligan	164

SECTION VI: TECHNOLOGY AND SCHOOL LEADERSHIP		**175**
20.	Innovative Learning Spaces: Design Thinking in Pedagogy Shwetangna Chakrabarty	177
21.	Technology in Today's Schools Todd Von Seggern	191
22.	Hit the Ground Running: Leveraging Distance Education for Teacher Induction Jeff Dungan	200

Index   210

Introduction
Innovative Leadership Practices in International Schools

Jayson W. Richardson

Perhaps more than any other sector of K–12 schooling, international schools have experienced unprecedented changes over the years. Technological advances, new understandings regarding curricular standards around the world, college/career-readiness, equity and social justice concerns, the globalization of human interactions, and economic competitiveness are all reshaping the work of international schools. These shifts are forcing international school leaders to reassess their schools' strengths and rethink the purposes, goals, and means by which they educate a diverse, complex, and ever-changing body of students. And, to do all this, they must work with a teaching faculty who are transnational, multilingual, and whose backgrounds include experiences in widely diverse cultures and educational systems. Encouragingly, the good work done in international schools is often directly applicable to many schools around the world. The focus of this book is on highlighting innovations in international schools *and* linking those to the leadership practices or mindsets that should and can occur in schools across the world.

This book is filled with examples of how leaders in international school initiate, sustain, and propel innovation in their unique contexts. Throughout, the reader will find experience-based contributions from leaders in international schools around the world. Rather than reporting research studies, the chapters capture the lived experiences of leaders within these unique contexts. This book contains many contributions that fall outside of the experiences of the Head of School in a desire to include voices of distributed leadership within these international learning organizations. Contributors are principals, assistant principals, curriculum directors, directors of technology integration, instructional coaches, media specialists, teacher leaders, and others.

The focus of the book is on innovation in schools. International schools are used as the lens; but each chapter concludes by highlighting lessons, strategies, and techniques that leaders of other schools can and should do to implement similar innovations. As a result, the book implicitly makes connections beyond international schools by exploring what can be learned from the exciting work being done in international schools. This link is made in each chapter under the heading "Innovative Leadership Practices."

Special Features of This Book

This book is intended to be a page-turner; the chapters are relatively short. Each one gives the reader just enough depth to understand the innovation or practice but is brief enough to be digested quickly and in one sitting. The intent is to capture the innovative practices currently happening in international schools, translate them into leadership actions, and show how they are played out in localized contexts.

To do this, there are a few special features of this book that will guide the reader. The first is the natural section breaks by categories which are detailed below. These categories were not predetermined but rather arose out of the open submission process. Thus, these sections are topical areas that might be most germane to international school leaders now.

The second feature is that each section contains a mixture of full chapters and vignettes. Full chapters are spaces for the author to go deeper into the nuances of how the innovation was initiated and is being sustained. These chapters are around 3000 words each. Sections also contain several vignettes. These vignettes serve to localize the innovation and tell a short story (around 1000 words) about that innovation in practice. Vignettes are not evenly distributed in the book, but rather appear in sections that are most relevant. For example, under *Student Agency*, there is one chapter and three vignettes. This may indicate that there are fewer formal innovations under this topic, yet innovative practices still exist.

The third special feature is that each chapter concludes with a paragraph on *Innovative Leadership Practices*. Here, the authors wrapped up their chapter by making links between school leadership and innovation. The authors used this concluding section to highlight practices that might be applied outside their specific context and even to other, non-international schools.

How This Book Is Organized

The contributions of this book fall into six broad categories, corresponding to the book's sections. *Student agency* is highlighted first. In this section, the authors address how structures and existing school cultures impact student voice, student choice, and student empowerment. The second section focuses on *equity* issues. The leaders highlighted here focus on issues of inclusion, international mindedness, and gender equity. The third section is focused on *curriculum, teaching, and learning*. Authors of these chapters focus on innovations such as shifting to skills-based exams, creating flexible curriculum structures, and adopting personal learning profiles for each student. The fourth section of the book addresses *school management* issues. The topics of implementing instructional coaching, refocusing school targets, rethinking innovative practices, and preparing leaders to academically investigate challenges in their unique contexts are found in this section. The fifth section highlights various facets of *teacher leadership*. It focuses on instructional leadership, distributed leadership, and action-oriented leadership. The sixth and final section is focused on *school technology and leadership*. Its chapters focus on repurposing space, improving teacher induction, and adopting ubiquitous technology across the curriculum.

Who Is This Book For?

This book is a value read for both academics and practitioners. The book highlights topics that are germane to international school leaders today, but the lessons are be applicable to *all* school leaders. International educators and leaders of international schools will benefit by better understanding current issues and cutting-edge practices that are relevant to this unique area of learning, teaching, and schooling. Non-international educators and school leaders will get a better understanding of cutting-edge educational innovations happening globally to determine how these practices might be adapted in local contexts. Pre-service teachers and leaders will benefit by using these chapters to ignite creative thinking and problem solving about schools, innovation, and leadership.

Summary

International schools do not get much press outside of their own stakeholder groups. University programs rarely focus content on the international school experience. The research conducted on international schools is often excluded from the mainstream discussion of educational innovation. This is likely due to the perception that international schools are a niche market. There is a misconception that lessons from international schools may not be germane to a larger audience. However, as detailed in our chapters, the stories and lessons learned are not idiosyncratic. The leadership lessons noted herein apply globally. By understanding what exciting things are happening in international schools around the world, the field of educational leadership is enriched (and hopefully inspired). By taking a global perceptive and applying it to a local context, the leadership lessons from these international schools can be translated to other stakeholder groups. I hope this book opens up the discussion and leads to a better understanding of the possibilities of innovation and school leadership.

Contributor Biographies

Glenda Baker is the High School Deputy Principal at UNIS Hanoi. Originally from Australia, Glenda has been passionate about student agency, organizational change, and coaching innovation throughout her career.

Joelle Basnight has served in six different international schools in the past 25 years. She is presently the High School Principal at the American International School Chennai.

Deborah Bradshaw has been an educator for over 20 years, trained initially in the U.K., and has worked in both inner city and rural schools. She has worked internationally in Malawi, Australia, Thailand, and Uganda. She is passionate about building inclusive communities.

Stephanie Budd received her Master of Education in Youth Development from the University of Illinois at Chicago and her Bachelor of Science in Biological Sciences from the University of Kentucky. Stephanie taught science at the Banjul American International School from 2016-2019 and previously designed and led educational programming at the Chicago Lights Urban Farm in Chicago, Illinois.

Shwetangna Chakrabarty is the IBDP coordinator at Guangzhou Nanfang International School in Guangzhou, China. She has over 12 years of experience in teaching three different curricula in four different countries. She has taught mathematics and business management to the International GCSE and the International Baccalaureate students. She has successfully handled multiple-responsibility positions including DP coordinator and pedagogical leader, Extended Essay Coordinator, MYP personal project

Contributor Biographies

coordinator, and CIS/NEASC accreditation coordinator. Apart from having a degree in education and an MBA, she is also a college counselor certified by TripleA learning, U.K. She loves to travel, sketches her experiences in her paintings, and avidly writes blogs which have been published by International Baccalaureate and The International Educator.

Kimberly Ann Cofino has been an educator in international schools since August 2000. Having lived and worked in Germany, Malaysia, Thailand, and Japan, Kim has had a variety of roles in international schools, including (her favorite) instructional coach. Now based in Bangkok, Thailand, Kim is the co-founder and CEO of Eduro Learning, author of *Your Connected Classroom: A Practical Guide for Teachers*, and the lead mentor and creator of the Eduro Learning The Coach mentorship microcredential program. Find out more about Kim at kimcofino.com.

John D'Arcy, D.Ed., taught in Toronto, Canada for 18 years before teaching internationally. In Toronto, John worked at a high school where 1150 students set their timetable, every day. For the past 13 years John has worked in international schools in Hong Kong, Istanbul, and Beijing. In Hong Kong John led the visioning and implementation of one of the first 1:1 laptop programs in Asia. In Istanbul, John led the school's work to make learning personal. John's doctoral research explored the impact of adaptive and mobile technologies on the personalization of learning. John, his wife Ida, and daughter Jade currently live in Beijing.

Jeff Dungan, Ed.D., is an Instructional Technology Coach at Shanghai American School. Jeff serves as an Instructional Designer and a Learning Design Coach at Global Online Academy and is a lead trainer for the ISTE Certified Educator program. Jeff holds a doctorate in instructional technology and distance education from Nova Southeastern University. His doctoral work focused on opinion leadership within East Asian International Schools and its role in the adoption of distance learning into traditional K-12 educational settings. Jeff has presented internationally on a variety of educational technology topics including computational thinking, reimagining innovative learning spaces, and diffusing innovations in K-12 schools. When not sitting in front of a screen Jeff relishes any opportunity to be on the water (or a beach) with his family kitesurfing, surfing and sailing throughout Southeast Asia.

Contributor Biographies

Jim Gerhard has been a teacher, vice-principal, principal, or school director in seven different countries over the past 21 years. He has worked in elementary, middle, and high schools and has always sought to improve and enrich the student experience in each overseas school.

Kristin Halligan is the principal of an early-years and primary school in Bangkok. She has been an international educator for over 15 years. She is an IB educator who serves on WASC accreditation committees. Her doctoral studies focused on changing school culture by building collaborative communities of practice. She is interested in parent participation and agency as well as creating connections between home and school.

Natasha Haque is currently a teacher coach working with educators across the Aga Khan Academies in Mombasa, Hyderabad and Maputo. She has been an IB Middle Years Programme coordinator and has spent time teaching in the UAE, Bahrain, Tanzania, and the U.K. She is passionate about promoting international mindedness and service learning. During her MEd Natasha earned an IB Advanced Certificate in teaching and learning for research work done on service learning. Natasha has presented and shared ideas at several IB conferences and written articles which have been published by IB Blogs and The International Educator. Natasha holds a Master's of Science in Development Studies from the School of Oriental and African Studies and a BA (Hons) Geography degree from the London School of Economics.

Ryan Elissa Hopkins-Wilcox is an international educator who has worked in Taiwan; Washington, D.C.; Cambodia; Uganda; and Kenya. Around the world she has inspired lifelong learning by igniting the power of passion and purpose for others. She works as a learning leader envisioning the future of education and realizing her dreams through her own journeys within the world of education.

Tosca Killoran has been teaching in the IB international community in Asia and Europe since 2000. She acts as an EDTech consultant to international schools as well as a presenter and keynote speaker at conferences and professional development sessions. She co-founded ED-ucation Publishing, founded TEDxYouth@BIS, TEDxYouth@NIST, and TEDxYouthJingshan in order to give greater voice to youth change-makers. She has written

14 children's books focused on global citizenship, service learning, and creating opportunities for learning communities to connect.

Jennifer D. Klein is a product of experiential project-based education. She taught high school and university English for 19 years, including 5 years in Central America and 11 in all-girls education. She has a broad background in global education, student-driven curricular strategies, single-sex education, student and teacher travel, intercultural inclusivity, and experiential, inquiry-driven learning. Jennifer is author of *The Global Education Guidebook: Humanizing K–12 Classrooms Worldwide Through Global Partnerships*, published in 2017. The same year, Jennifer became Head of School at Gimnasio Los Caobos outside of Bogotá, Colombia. As a school leader, author, speaker, and bilingual workshop facilitator, Jennifer strives to inspire educators to shift their practices in schools worldwide.

Kristen L. MacConnell, Ph.D., is passionate about bringing innovative teaching and leadership practices to schools. Her career as an educator spans 20 years. Her roles have ranged from early intervention teacher to school leader. Kristen worked at the International School Nido de Aguilas for six years. She currently serves as the Director of the Teacher Training Center for international school educators.

Gray Macklin has been working in education since 1999, first in Georgia and then in Seoul since 2006. Having just made the transition to administration in 2017, Gray is continuing to learn how to stay involved with students in a meaningful way while keeping up with office work.

Matthew Militello is the founding faculty member of the East Carolina University International Ed.D. He is a former middle and high public school teacher, assistant principal, and principal. He has more than 75 publications, including six co-authored books. He has received more than $14 million in external funding to conduct professional development and research for K–12 school leaders.

Christie Powell has served as an international educator and leader for over 20 years in IB, American, and international schools in Africa and Asia. Her journey through education has included teaching from elementary through university, director roles in curriculum, assessment and professional development, and the principalship. She has served as a site chair for WASC/CIS as well as a literacy consultant. Her doctoral studies focused on cultural and linguistic responsiveness in curriculum development and teacher inquiry to increase student engagement and learning.

Jayson W. Richardson is an Associate Professor at the University of Kentucky in the USA. Jayson's research, teaching, and service links school technology leadership and future-ready school leadership. Jayson is the Director of the Center for the Advanced Study of Technology Leadership in Education (CASTLE). He is the Co-Editor in Chief for the *Journal of Educational Administration*. Jayson has written or co-authored nearly 90 articles and book chapters. Jayson's work appears in journals such as: *Comparative Education Review, Educational Administration Quarterly, International Journal of Education and Development using ICT, Information Technology for International Development, Journal of International Development, Journal of School Leadership, Review of Policy Research*, and *The Teacher Educator*.

Elizabeth Rossini, Ph.D., is an education consultant who has been working nationally and internationally in the areas of curriculum, assessment, and instruction for the past 19 years. Her school-based experience spans pre-kindergarten to university and includes teaching, instructional technology, curriculum, professional learning, and both school and central office administration. She has taken a break from full-time consulting to work for the past six years at International School Bangkok as the Director of Curriculum and Professional Learning. After a wonderful experience at International School Bangkok Elizabeth has transitioned to The Nueva School as the Director of Teaching and Learning.

Sarah Ssengendo has 16 years of experience teaching children in elementary schools. She has lived and worked in the United Kingdom, Uganda, Romania, and Tanzania. She will be taking on the role of Primary Years Programme Coordinator next year in her current school.

Caleb Steindam has spent 16 years in education as a teacher, teacher educator, and educational administrator. He was Director of the Banjul American International School from 2016-2019 and is a doctoral candidate in curriculum and instruction at Loyola University Chicago.

Daniel Todd is a British-born educator with 15 years of experience in international education. He is passionate about learner-centered learning, learning communities, and co-creating a vision of learning for this century.

Lynda Tredway worked closely with Matt Militello to create and implement the East Carolina University International Ed.D. She is Senior Associate at the Institute for Educational Leadership in Washington, D.C. and was founding director of the Principal Leadership Institute (PLI) at the University of California Berkeley's Graduate School of Education (2000-2012). Tredway and Militello were recently awarded $9.7 million from the U.S. Department of Education to work with school leaders to improve academic discourse in STEM courses.

Todd Von Seggern currently works at the International School of Uganda as the technology integrator and instructional coach. Todd promotes learning between teachers and students through agency and inquiry, believing that we all are learners who need to pursue our passions. Throughout his career, Todd has used technology to empower teachers and students to ignite their love for learning.

SECTION 1

Student Agency

Introduction to Section I: Student Agency

Student agency is a topic gaining much traction these days. There is much talk about student voice, student, choice, student empowerment, and student engagement. At the core of these discussions is the notion of agency. Hence, this section explores how student agency is often a focus in international schools. This focus requires a leader who fully understands that the purpose of schooling is to serve students and support their individual growth in a number of ways.

The first section of this book is focused on student agency. In this section, there is one full chapter and a series of vignettes that exemplify student agency in action. The first contribution is from Glenda Baker who focused on how her school in Hanoi, Vietnam focused on empowering students by modifying the schedule. In Chapter 1, Glenda provides examples of how the leadership worked with teachers to create exploration courses that allowed students to be agents of their own learning. This chapter also lays out the leadership decisions that had to occur before this flexible scheduling took hold. In Chapter 2, Shwetangna Chakrabarty and Natasha Haque wrote a vignette entitled "Classrooms Without Teachers." Here the authors provide examples of how one school rethought student choice and voice. In this Tanzanian school, the leaders allow students to identify topics that they want to study and even allow students to take the lead in the instruction of that topic. In Chapter 3, Kristen MacConnell wrote a vignette linking play and design thinking. By using design thinking principles, Kristin and her team were able to reinvigorate the playground by allowing students, parents, and teachers to have a voice. In Chapter 4, Sara Ssengendo presents how her school, located in Uganda, created structures and outlets to foster student creativity by supporting personal learning journeys.

Innovative leadership practices evident in this section on student agency are plentiful. School leaders must create space for teachers and students to engage in deeper learning experiences and foster opportunities for students to practice critical skill development. Empowering and supporting teachers to guide curriculum development, in ways often divergent from the norm, is also necessary. Distributed leadership was evident throughout this section. Be it giving teachers free reign to build new courses, giving teachers the opportunity to rethink spaces where kids play, or allowing staff to engage in their own learning journey, sharing leadership matters! Student agency, after all, is about creating creative, thriving, and empowered students who can navigate the uncertain paths that lie ahead.

iBlock @ UNIS Hanoi: Turning Potential into Performance

Glenda Baker

> **Summary**
>
> This chapter discusses how one international school allocated time in the school day for students to engage in learning that prioritizes skill development and interdisciplinary learning within the context of current topics and areas of student interest. It includes a discussion of the design process and how school leaders empowered teachers and students to define course structure, outcomes, and assessment methods. The chapter includes examples of course titles and descriptions that the school introduced in the first year along with some of the leadership lessons learned throughout the process.

When students are empowered to direct their learning, they become masters of their future and their potential. *iBlock* was introduced to support students to explore and expand their interests and expand their knowledge of contemporary topics while building skills and confidence as learners. For students to develop agency and to respond actively to their circumstances, they need opportunities to practice self-direction. Students with agency "tend to seek meaning and act with purpose to achieve the conditions they desire in their own and others' lives" (Ferguson, Phillips, Rowley, & Friedlander, 2015, p. 1). At United Nations International School of Hanoi, we created time in the school day for students to develop and practice these essential skills while pursuing and discovering new passions and interests.

The United Nations International School of Hanoi turned 30 in 2018 and has grown considerably since it opened as the first international school in the city. The school currently has around 1120 students from Discovery (age 3) to Grade 12, coming from more than 67 different countries. We are a school aspiring to live the values of the United Nations and we are a learning community that is unique and distinctive.

The school's mission, vision, and values reflect shared beliefs that our school should help students become independent lifelong learners, who feel equipped to create a better world. United Nations International School of Hanoi is an International Baccalaureate World School. Students entering elementary follow the Primary Years Programme (PYP). At Grade 6, students begin the Middle Years Programme (MYP) which concludes in Grade 10. Students typically undertake the Diploma Programme (DP) for Grade 11 and 12. A problem that leaders of the school were grappling with was how to create time and focus for students to grow beyond the curriculum. As school leaders, we wanted to know how to turn student potential, identified through interests, passions, and independent inquiry, into performance across social, emotional, and academic settings.

Evaluating School Structures for How Well They Support Student Agency

A question that teachers and administrators were grappling with was how to create conditions for deeper student engagement by nurturing student interests and self-direction. A team of teachers was tasked with exploring how the schedule was helping or hindering this outcome. Questions that were being asked included *Is the schedule dictating the kinds of teaching and learning that students experience?* and *What kinds of skills do all students need time to practice to live fulfilling and balanced lives?* Middle and high students were tightly scheduled and there was limited opportunity during the school day for self-directed or interest-based learning. Furthermore, attempts to integrate a truly interdisciplinary learning experience, which is an MYP requirement, lacked a systematic approach.

What could teachers and students achieve in a 20-hour learning experience, which is approximately one quarter? We began the design process by defining a nine-week course structure. Nine weeks was enough time to dig into a topic, but short enough to maintain momentum and interest. We settled on a plan for classes to meet four times in a ten-day cycle. *iBlock* would include two different courses, *Explorations* and *Interdisciplinary* courses.

The design team wanted student voice to inform the courses that would be offered. Early in the planning, middle and high school students were canvassed for ideas that helped teachers come up with options under either an *Interdisciplinary* or an *Exploration* course. Using student ideas, teachers then collaborated to create titles and descriptions. Arts and humanities teachers were enlisted to help build on student-generated ideas. MYP guidelines note schools must provide a minimum of 50 hours per year to teaching a subject. A reduction in contact hours for arts and humanities courses was decided upon because that was where the interdisciplinary units had typically fallen, albeit in an inconsistent way. This also created teacher availability. While initially this decision made sense to everyone involved, after courses began some teachers expressed concerns feeling like they have "lost" time. This continues to be an area for thought and discussion.

Everyone agreed that *iBlock* courses should incorporate project-based learning and should highlight the value of skills development as a priority alongside concepts and experience. We recognized that some of the most critical skills for all learners to master include collaboration, and critical and creative thinking (World Economic Forum, 2018). With these ideas in mind, the development team, made up of teachers and leadership, proposed the following objectives and aspirational outcomes to guide teachers as they envisioned possible courses. *iBlock* courses would support students to:

- make choices about their learning
- engage with authentic, real-world tasks that interest them and develop a positive attitude to learning
- explore a diversity of experiences and approaches
- plan what they will do by setting short-term goals and success criteria
- deepen their ability to apply skills in new contexts
- develop "future-ready" dispositions
- develop skills (communication, social, research, self-management, thinking)

Explorations have a focus on skill building and include topics such as first aid and sound engineering that students expressed interest in pursuing. *Explorations* incorporate student goal setting within the scope of the topic and use self-assessment and student reflection as part of the assessment and reporting process. *Interdisciplinary* courses address topics that draw on at least two different subject areas (e.g., the course *Is the Future Post-Human?* explores science and social studies concepts.) *Interdisciplinary* courses align with the MYP guidelines and are assessed using the MYP interdisciplinary criteria. Students select three *Explorations* and one *Interdisciplinary* course to undertake over a school year to make up their *iBlock* experience. *iBlock* courses are reported to parents and appear on a student's school transcript. Table 1.1 and Table 1.2 provide an overview of course titles and descriptions for both *Explorations* and *Interdisciplinary* courses that were offered for student sign-up in the first year of *iBlock*.

Table 1.1 Examples of high school explorations courses

Speech "Finding Your Voice"
Explore three different skills of speaking including public speaking, debating and informal speaking. Learn skills to enhance your vocal and nonverbal communication techniques. Gain confidence in all types of situations to have your ideas heard.

CSI Hanoi: Forensics
Learn about and apply forensic science concepts and skills as a variety of crime scenes are investigated and "solved"; this exploration could provide opportunities for research as well as application of technology and probeware.

Game Design with Unity
Using the Unity game engine to create 2D/3D worlds that can be explored and interacted with. You will learn the programming concepts of variables, loops, conditionals, and objects in the language of C#.

First Responders: First Aid
Build your ability as a skilled first aid responder by acquiring emergency first aid skills and understandings leading to an American Red Cross first aid certification.

Sports Science
Use engineering design principles to explore a variety sports science technology; this exploration could provide opportunities for investigation, design, building, and evaluation of sports science technology.

Table 1.2 Examples of high school interdisciplinary courses

UNESCO World Heritage
Learn more about UNESCO world heritage sites around the world and specifically here in Vietnam. You will investigate the UNESCO world heritage criteria and consider the impact on UNESCO sites caused by human development.

Finance & Investment
Learn a range of strategies from everyday finance to high-end investment to build equity toward being a fiscally responsible individual who knows how to make and save money.

Life After War
How does a culture heal after war and extreme violence? How does the human psyche deal with the repercussions? In this unit, we will explore cultural artifacts and texts created with the mindset of recovery and reconciliation and whether this is even possible.

Zombie Apocalypse
Could you survive a Zombie Apocalypse? Why are people so obsessed with zombies? Learn about the science of disease outbreaks, as well as the mythology of zombies through art, film, and literature.

Is the Future Post-Human?
Learn to think like a futurist! You will investigate the impact that scientific and technological innovation have on humanity, how artists and innovators are reimagining and predicting our future.

We brought together a team of teachers to envision the self-assessment process for *Explorations*. The team identified five skill areas from a much longer list of Approaches to Learning (ATLs) from the International Baccalaureate (i.e., communication, social, research, self-management, and critical/creative thinking). Students now self-assess using levels from *Novice* to *Learner* to *Practitioner* to *Expert*. The self-assessment process includes students explaining their level in the context of their decisions and actions during the course. At the beginning of an *Exploration* course, students select two or three skills to focus on which are relevant to their learning and project goals. At the end of the course, students reflect on their progress with their teacher and submit a comment that supported the level they achieved.

The feedback on the self-assessment process and taking an intentional focus on skills has been positive. As one teacher explained, "I can see that this approach is helping the students self-reflect. I think the kids are getting better at seeing their own goals. Focusing on the skills has been quite different. It has incorporated the 'how' not just the 'what' in an important way. I think spending time talking about 'how' you do something—the process—is having an impact."

To help students move between *Exploration* courses to know what to expect, teachers agreed to follow a similar structure. Courses begin with teacher-led learning experiences related to the topic. This lasts for around three weeks. Students are then guided to define a goal to extend their learning in an area of interest within the topic. Part of the goal setting includes making it both challenging and achievable with the timeframe. Students then identify two or three skills they want to develop that are well matched to their goal. Teachers play active coaching and consulting roles. Students revisit their goals, their success criteria, and the skills they chose over the remaining six weeks. Near the end of the course, students evaluate their skills and goals using a common self-assessment rubric. Students also post a narrative about their goal and learning in the online gradebook. This allows parents to see reflection and feedback.

Teachers came together periodically to discuss strategies for goal setting and self-assessment, and to share how they are teaching specific skills. These meetings helped colleagues uncover common concerns and provide insights to us about what is working. As one teacher explained, "What I like is that the conversations with students about skills in *iBlock* are having an impact on my other classes. We are much more explicit, and we talk about the skills rather than the content. For me, self-management was the one skill that has been particularly highlighted. Students are starting to explicitly use the language in both contexts: my iBlock course and my music classes."

We hoped to reduce teacher wear and tear by running each *iBlock* course four times in a year with the same teacher. This would mean a teacher could develop the course and then reteach it multiple times, reducing their preps and providing a more rapid refinement timeframe. Unfortunately, some courses did not receive enough student interest to run for all four quarters. This meant several teachers had to design and teach more than one course. Several teachers who were supporters and advocates for *Explorations* started feeling burnt-out and raised concerns about teaching loads. "On top of developing a new topic, it feels like I'm back at the start of the school year, starting all over with a new group of students while colleagues are continuing on with their year-long courses." Some teachers who had been asked to design courses in the development stage, left the school or were needed to teach other courses. The result was that we had to ask different teachers to teach courses they had not helped design. Some teachers found it a challenge to pick up course plans that some else had envisioned while others did not feel completely confident about some topics.

An ongoing leadership challenge has been to help teachers understand that equity does not always mean equality. Perceptions are powerful and left unaddressed lead to discontent and resentment. To support teachers, we continued to listen with empathy and seek input on ways we reduce pain points while keeping students as our focus. One strategy we will try next year is to manage the student request process differently. The trade-off may be to slightly limit student choice but create more certainty for teachers.

As teachers become more comfortable and confident that students can, and want, to drive their own learning, we anticipate fewer teacher-designed and -directed learning tasks and more student-initiated experiences. Three directions we hope to explore in the future include introducing:

1. topics that feature a clearer connection to our commitment to the United Nations Strategic Development Goals,
2. topics that make use of online learning opportunities, and
3. using *iBlock* to cater to different learning needs such as English Language Learners and students who would benefit from enrichment and extension opportunities.

Without a doubt, the change process for creating *iBlock* has been messy and uncomfortable. It is still a work-in-progress. In his article *Leading Change: Why Transformation Efforts Fail*, John Kotter (1995) outlined eight steps that leaders need to pay attention to for successful management of a new initiative. As we look at some of our decisions about those steps, it could be argued that as leaders we made simple blunders and missed some important opportunities in the rollout of *iBlock*. Below is a review of some of Kotter's key steps and reflections on what we might have done differently, or got right.

Leadership decisions and lessons learned:

- *Establishing the need and a sense of urgency.* The creation of *iBlock* was only one part of bigger scheduling decisions that were made at the school. Schedule changes are always political, so the reason for disruption must be student-centered and compelling. There is still debate within the leadership team about if the current schedule is the best we could do.

- *Enlisting and maintaining a strong team to drive the change.* Some of the people who were enthusiastic leaders of *iBlock* left the school midway through the implementation process. This resulted in a loss of momentum. We then needed to enlist new teachers who had not had the same initial level of commitment or sense of urgency. As a result, nurturing teacher-leadership has become a strategic focus.

- *Creating and sharing the vision.* Feedback from Grade 10 students helped us see that we had not communicated enough about aspects of the change. Some students felt they had lost time in an important subject. Students were unaware that the new stand-alone interdisciplinary course had previously been covered during their humanities course. How teachers explained the change in hours to their classes had also contributed to this confusion. This was a misunderstanding that could have been avoided with clearer and more timely communication.

- *Communicating the vision.* We hosted information sessions for parents, teachers, and students to inform and explain the new schedule and goals of *iBlock*. We have begun to include parent newsletter articles about *iBlock* courses that include student comments.

- *Empowering people to act on the vision.* During the initial course design process, a team of teachers was assigned to create topics before staffing decisions being finalized. This was not an empowering process for the teachers who ended up being asked to teach a topic that had a lot of student interest, but they had not collaborated on. We have learned how important it is to give teachers agency over the *iBlock* course they will teach.

- *Planning short-term win.* We permitted teachers to adjust along the way. Making incremental changes in response to observations and feedback has helped us create goodwill and provide positive conditions for the next year's courses.

- *Consolidate learning and set longer-term goals.* Time will tell if *iBlock*, in its current form, will be retained in the school's ongoing program. Much has been learned with further reflection needed before more changes are made. In the meantime, *iBlock* has provided students with new learning opportunities and a fresh focus on skills and has encouraged teachers to incorporate more student self-assessment as evidence of learning.

Innovative Leadership Practices

The innovation practices highlighted in this chapter included how we created time and space for students to learn and practice critical skills. United Nations International School of Hanoi is intentionally focusing on the value of key lifelong skills such as communication, social skills, thinking, and research. Incorporating student-self assessment must not be treated merely as a nice add-on but as the key process for students to identify and celebrate their learning. This is a step toward trusting students to oversee their own learning.

A key leadership practice that has been discussed in this chapter centers on how to create conditions that empower and support teachers and students to make decisions about teaching and learning. Making information freely available, being inclusive, and taking time to explain how decisions are made can help build trust and confidence. Above all else, having empathy and being able to understand and acknowledge how teachers and students experience innovation can help move ideas forward.

References

Farrington, C., Roderick, M., Allensworth, E, Nagaoka, J. Keyes, T., Johnson, D., & Beechum, N. (2012). *Teaching adolescents to become learners: The role of noncognitive factors in shaping school performance: A critical literature review*. Chicago, IL: University of Chicago.

Ferguson, R. F., Phillips, S. F., Rowley, J. F. S., & Friedlander, J. W. (2015) *The influence of teaching beyond standardized test scores: Engagement, mindsets, and agency*. Cambridge, MA: The Achievement Gap Initiative at Harvard University.

International Baccalaureate (n.d.). *Approaches to learning in the International Baccalaureate (IB) Diploma Programme*. Retrieved from https://www.ibo.org/globalassets/digital-tookit/flyers-and-artworks/approaches-to-teaching-learning-dp-en.pdf

Kotter, J. P. (1995). Leading change: Why transformation efforts fail. *Harvard Business Review*, 1–9. Retrieved from https://eoeleadership.hee.nhs.uk/sites/default/files/leading_change_why_transformation_efforts_fail.pdf

World Economic Forum (2016). *The future of jobs: Employment, skills, and workforce strategy for the Fourth Industrial Revolution*. Retrieved from http://www3.weforum.org/docs/WEF_Future_of_Jobs.pdf

 Vignette: Classrooms Without Teachers

Shwetangna Chakrabarty and Natasha Haque

> **Summary**
>
> In this vignette, we provide examples of how one school rethought borders. Examples include rethinking content borders as well as borders between the digital and analog worlds.

Leading Your Own Learning

Every year in our Individuals and Societies (humanities) classrooms, students in Grades 6 through 10 begin their learning by designing their own units using the IB Middle Years Programme framework. They identify the concepts, context, and topics that they would like to study. After designing their topics of study, they pitch their ideas to the entire class. Those ideas are then voted upon and, in the upper grades, students actually teach a few lessons of their unit!

The fascinating thing about the choices that our students make is that they rarely match conventional humanities topics. Students often are naturally drawn to learn more about their personal histories and geographies. This has led to students researching and proposing units about the contribution of former colonies to the World Wars from the perspective of colonial troops, or researching issues in their immediate environment (e.g., poaching). When students go through the pitching process, it leads them to inquire and question about who decides the history that we learn in schools and which perspectives dominate and which are hidden. Students also get a taste of planning and driving their learning.

Learning in the Cloud

From the boundaries of a classroom to the vast expanse of the internet, learning can take place seamlessly if led by the learner. Usually, school projects are structured and led by the teacher but, at our school, our students have created their cloud classroom using the collaborative Google Office Suite.

The first step our students took was to deconstruct the IB guides in order to then reconstruct their own digital guide. The role of the teacher is to facilitate them in this process. The inspiration for this initiative came from an assessment of the varied student needs in the class. With a majority of students in the class either on an Individual Learning Plan (ILP) or an Individual Educational Plan (IEP), as curriculum coordinators we had to decide to take a risk and create a new space that would be more flexible and open, allowing for closer monitoring of student progress. Our journey of moving projects to the Google Drive platform began.

The purpose of recreating the IB Personal Project guide was to ensure that students read through the various elements and requirements and can articulate it in their own words. Previously, the guide was recreated by a teacher to make it more student friendly. This new approach, however, meant that the students designed their own learning process. As each project is individualized, it allowed for differentiated collaboration between the student and the teacher. The students also kept a digital version of the process journal that was shared with supervisors eliminating the need to meet face to face for feedback.

During the entire process, students learned digital etiquette, efficient citation, and ways to avoid academic misconduct. Supervisors could vary instruction via flipped classroom strategies. With the reports being written continuously throughout product development, there was a clear connection between the planning and action.

Under our leadership, the cloud classroom helped create the bridge between the middle school and high school, since the resources, tools, and structures can be well aligned for all criterion-based assessments, allowing for seamless transitions between programs at the grade levels. Within these technology-enabled learning spaces, we can bridge the gap between approaches to teaching and approaches to learning, thus allowing teachers to be mentors.

> ## Innovative Leadership Practices
>
> What connects both of these examples is that students felt empowered to lead their teaching and learning. As curriculum leaders, our experience was also enriched, because we have seen positive results through innovative leadership practices spearheaded by both of us. These experiences have convinced us that the magic of learning happens when students guide their learning journey. Our success with these innovative leadership practices has motivated our teachers to plan differently and made our students better advocates for their preferred learning styles.

Vignette: Innovate, Play, Transform: Design Thinking in the Early Years

Kristen L. MacConnell

> **Summary**
>
> This vignette describes how teachers from the Early Years School at Nido de Aguilas used a design thinking process to create a more engaging play environment while working within a small budget. The team took time to deeply understand the problem before jumping to solutions. A clear goal was set regarding student outcomes, one central to all decision making: helping school leaders prioritize needs based on both feasibility and usefulness toward achieving the goal.

Young children love to climb. My first 30 minutes on the playground as the new Assistant Director of the Early Years School (EYS) at Nido de Aguilas confirmed this notion. Children were climbing up low fences, climbing on playhouses, and climbing up stacks of tires. I scanned the playground for toys and noticed another problem: There were none. The balls had been thrown or kicked over the fence. The hula hoops, cones, and sand toys were broken. By the end of the first month of school our children had limited toys for play.

I invited teachers to join a playground committee in September. We had a small budget of $8000 USD. There was not enough funds for major structural changes but with some creativity and innovation, I knew we could make an impact. During our first 30-minute meeting eight teachers gathered to discuss our challenges. Everyone had ideas for improvement.

Before we jumped to solutions, however, it was important to deeply understand our problem.

We worked together to craft a problem statement: "Our playground lacks a variety of equipment and intentional materials to cultivate the physical and social development of our students." Next, we brainstormed factors contributing to the problem: lack of equipment variety, not maximizing the available space, low-quality materials, and the need to create more opportunities for children to practice sharing and problem solving.

By the end of the meeting we had mapped our problem. Before our next meeting, we agreed to interview 3–4 colleagues about their experiences supervising outdoor play. I agreed to elicit student feedback. We also decided to keep a "bug list" for one week recording notes about things that "bugged" us on the playground.

Three weeks later we met to share our findings. Teacher data revealed that the biggest challenges on the playground were: helping children to solve conflicts; tidying up at the end of recess; creating opportunities for students to climb, swing, and balance; and creating more opportunities for water play. The children wanted more things to climb, more toys for make-believe, a track to ride tricycles, a giant playhouse, and teeter totters. Next we shared our "bug lists." Examples from the bug lists included: Toys don't stimulate play, toys are not high-quality, sand is in places not meant for play, art center is uninspiring, and the big box/shed in the tricycle area takes up space for play.

Based on user-generated data, we set a goal to create a fun, innovative, and creative playground that fosters children's play. With our problem defined and our goal set, we got to work. We began a five-minute rapid brainstorm where we generated as many ideas as possible. Committee members rated ideas on a scale of 1 to 10 based on two criteria: (1) usefulness in addressing our problem and (2) feasibility given our budget. We summed up the total score for each idea and then used the scores to prioritize our needs in relation to our goal.

The final task of the committee was to seek parent input. We offered a 90-minute design thinking challenge for parents to reimagine our outdoor space. Our parents worked in small groups to prototype some possible playground designs. At the semester's end, the principal and I used the data to create a final plan for our mini redesign. Our biggest expense was redesigning a covered play space that had three walls and opened to our lower play area. This space was currently unused by children. The floor was uneven and the space often flooded with rain. A deck built to even out the surface solved our flooding issue. The new space became an area for creative play. We painted one wall with chalkboard paint and added tables with games and art supplies, PVC pipes for building and creating, a water table, an outdoor kitchen, and dress-up clothes for dramatic play.

We had two existing wooden playhouses. Our maintenance staff reinforced the houses for structural safety and improved them by closing in the framing (which children used to climb). This area became a small town. We added large blocks for building and parking spots for the tricycles. Finally, in our upper play area we added logs as balance beams in an open grassy field.

Innovative Leadership Practices

It is often easier to make top-down decisions as a leader. However, dedicating time to a process which allows teachers to work collaboratively yields lasting solutions. Keeping a child-centered goal in my mind while making decisions helps tackle problems in a meaningful way. We used tools from High Tech High's Graduate School of Education (fishbone diagram protocol), from the Stanford d.School (empathy interviews), and from NoTosh's design thinking process (bug lists). These protocols helped facilitate a process in which every voice was heard and valued.

Vignette: Developing Creativity in Schools

Sarah Ssengendo

> **Summary**
>
> At the International School of Uganda, everyone is seen as a learner. The leadership team provide the structures required to allow staff to pursue Personal Learning Journeys with their students. The following is an account of one such journey.

When several of my Grade 4 students set goals to "improve their creativity" or "get more creative," I found myself asking these questions: What is creativity? Can it be learned? Can it be measured? While I did read books, blogs, and watch videos, I quickly realized that my most valuable source of information was my students. Together we surveyed the school community. While many found it difficult to define "creativity," a fairly typical response was "Some people are creative. They can draw and paint well." Following this, we explored what creativity looked like through different subject lenses and developed the following definition: Creativity is using our imagination, choosing our best ideas, and then making good use of them.

We started a discussion wall where a provocation would be posted, and ideas graffitied around it. Provocations included images, an article, or a question such as: How can we encourage more children to play on the big field? How can we better organize our furniture/stationery? To what extent do people in this community work together? Can we be more carbon-neutral? As the students contributed their ideas, they were encouraged to respond to other comments, write questions, make connections, and elaborate on ideas. Walls slowly developed over the weeks.

Collaborative problem solving, essential for developing creativity, allowed us to think together. I noticed that those students who rarely contributed to the discussion were often at the wall writing. I used cognitive modeling a lot, to begin with. For example: "Oh, this is a good idea from Amy. It is similar to Abdullah's. I don't think string would work though. I wonder how we could make that better? Maybe using bottle tops and wire? Hmm, I'll try to draw it here." End products for us included student-designed learning spaces, mixed-gender football at break times, a student-initiated flower garden, and innovative model eco-houses. We have taken this idea out into the corridors where the wider community can contribute.

During one of our units, we inquired into how historical evidence tells us about the past. Some of our math and language benchmarks included: make accurate observations; infer meaning; use prepositions; form opinions based on evidence; measure length and weight; collect, record, and analyze data; and use coordinates and directional language. Provocations and challenges were intentionally teacher-designed to allow the students to become archeologists, lab scientists, mapmakers, historians, display designers, and museum curators through researching, making artifacts, and opening a museum to the community. The students were given lots of choice, voice, and ownership. I learned to let go and give them time to reflect and adapt. Teaching in this way is an art. It is a much messier process. However, through a carefully integrated creative curriculum, students can learn content, skills, and attitudes in authentic, creative ways that motivate them to become advocates of their own learning.

Along the way, I realized that in order to assess creativity, I must be clear on what specifically is being targeted. I started making sure that my shared lesson objectives included skills and dispositions as well as the content. I observed my students, more than ever before, enabling me to design purposeful future learning experiences. My evidence of learning included videos, graffiti walls, written reflections, notes, checklists, and rubrics. As the year went on, the students themselves became better at assessing and documenting their learning.

My aim had been to learn about creativity, which I did. But I also learned about learning and environment. Great ideas usually come to us when we are relaxed. Therefore, it is imperative that schools create relaxed, socially supportive learning environments where all thoughts can be freely expressed and are valued. I was reminded to value effort above outcome, process above product, and to see mistakes as learning opportunities. Next year I will be taking on a leadership role, and I aim to remember the importance of creativity. As a leader, I will encourage teachers to take risks and to be innovators within their classrooms, ensure the curriculum changes to stay relevant, integrated, and creative, make time for staff to collaborate in order to share ideas and perspectives and to problem-solve, and ensure the continuation of staff Personal Learning Journeys.

Innovative Leadership Practices

Children are naturally creative. As educators, we should give them the freedom to continue being so. We do not know what the future will be like. However, our children will need to be able to feel, understand, think, and cooperate. They will need to make thoughtful choices, develop sustainable solutions, and innovate. Creativity should, therefore, form an essential part of every child's education. As educators, we need to find ways to get students connecting emotionally and working collaboratively in order to get creative thinking happening in our schools.

Educators need creativity in today's schools. Leaders must think seriously about how to find the time and space for collaborative, creative thinking between staff members. Are teachers given the time and freedom to be courageous and innovative? Does the curriculum honor authentic learning, engage diverse learners, and spark innovation? In this transformation era in education, school leadership must put minds together, upturn long-held educational assumptions, and foster environments where creativity can flourish.

SECTION II

Equity

Introduction to Section II: Equity

Issues of equity are at the forefront of many educational conversations. The notion of creating a system that supports every child and honors the diversity of the individual is usually bedrock to most leaders. Yet how this gets done is a challenge with which many leaders struggle. Equity can wear many hats and might include gender, ability, identity, and culture. In this section, authors present how their schools are innovating around issues of equity.

This section begins with Chapter 5 written by Ryan Ellis Hopkins-Wilcox and Deborah Bradshaw. The focus of this chapter is on inclusion. Ryan and Deborah lay out exactly how the International School of Uganda adopted a model of inclusion that was applied across the school. The authors provide a step-by-step action plan detailing how they made this happen. Natasha Haque focuses Chapter 6 on international-mindedness. This concept is ever-changing for leaders of schools who may have upwards of 100 nationalities represented between the student and teaching bodies. Natasha shares her experiences in two schools, where school leaders and stakeholders conducted curriculum audits to determine how to enhance international mindedness, as defined in these unique contexts. Chapter 7 focuses on a project titled "Women in Science." Here, Stephanie Budd and Caleb Steindam detail how this West African school partnered with organization in the community to allow students to explore how women have, and are, contributing to the field of science.

In this section, the authors provided concrete examples of innovative practices related to how their schools espoused equity. Time and again, a theme that arose from these chapters was about moving the school culture away from compliance and toward innovation and meaningful change. This starts with creating a shared understanding and giving voice to multiple perspectives, be it from teachers, staff, students, or parents. Equity might also include a shift from traditional practices and toward the promotion of real-world interactions.

A Journey to Inclusion

Ryan Elissa Hopkins-Wilcox and Deborah Bradshaw

Summary

This chapter charts how the International School of Uganda embarked on a journey to make a learning support model more inclusive. The chapter shares insights into how a school might develop an action plan to help them implement inclusion or any new innovation. Our journey recognizes the guidance that eminent authors and coaches can provide as well as giving a "roadmap" for how one school enacted change within their context. The chapter concludes with hopes and dreams for the future of learning and some *what if* statements that might guide schools to consider their own beliefs and actions about learning.

 ## Why Inclusion?

> Do schools reflect society, or do schools transform society?
> ~ Next Frontier Inclusion (2014)

Our journey toward inclusion takes place in Kampala, at the International School of Uganda (ISU). ISU is a small International Baccalaureate school. There are 250 students within the elementary school (ages 2 to 11), with a variety of nationalities, languages, cultures, strengths, and stories. As a school we always celebrated these differences, but we wanted to do more than just acknowledge diversity, we wanted to transform beliefs about

25

Equity

diversity and inclusion. This story is told by one of our learning support teachers and the elementary assistant principal. The innovation shared in this story is grounded in the belief that inclusion can transform society into a place where differences are acknowledged and celebrated as strengths and each individual contributes to the collective well-being of all.

How do we build an inclusive school?

We did not know how to build an inclusive school. But we can now look back on the steps we took and share these as a guide for other schools on the same journey. First, let us define for you what we mean by inclusion. We have been able to shape a definition of inclusive learning as:

> We believe that inclusion is a holistic approach that serves to provide barrier-free, strength-based access to all learners and to facilitate solutions that enhance the learning environment.

If you are looking to follow steps, be aware that our journey to inclusion took the team one year of weekly meetings and school-wide gatherings to plan. Then a second year to implement including meetings and time to revise and restructure our plan as we worked through it. We are now in the third year of this journey. The team that worked on this innovation comprised teacher representatives from early childhood (ages 2.5 to 6), lower elementary (ages 6 to 8), and upper elementary (ages 8 to 11); a teacher from a specialist subject area (e.g., additional languages); a learning support teacher; the elementary assistant principal; and the elementary principal.

Examine Current Reality

We began with an audit of the current reality of our learning support services to help us to understand where we were and begin thinking about where we wanted to be (see Table 5.1). We used the document "Towards Inclusion: Planning Our Path: An Inclusive Audit Protocol" by NFI (2013) to help determine our current reality. This encouraged us to identify the barriers to address in order to match our emerging philosophy to our practice. We

Table 5.1 Current reality audit

Findings	Inquiries
There is no shared philosophy or policy for learning support.	How can shared expectations guided our actions in ways that are aligned to current best practice and pedagogy?
There are not enough staff members in learning support.	How can we be creative with the staffing we have to maximize the potential of learning support? Can we increase staffing?
The environments are not fully supportive of inclusion.	How can we remove barriers to learning in our physical spaces and our timetables?
Documentation is not supporting collaboration or learning.	How can we improve upon our systems for pedagogical documentation for learning support?
Teachers are hesitant to be "inclusive."	How can we build capacity and understanding in our team to feel competent and capable as inclusive educators?
Learning support, English as an additional language, counseling, and nursing are all their own departments, physically and mentally removed from the general elementary school.	How can we build a collaborative space and team for inclusion?
Not all students are being identified or receiving support that reflects best practice.	How can we better know our children and support their strengths and challenges?
The learning support assistants (LSA) are employed by the families and therefore are not necessarily highly qualified, nor a part of the learning support or ISU team.	Do we need LSAs? What is their role? What is ISU's role in ensuring quality instruction is delivered to every child?
Students are sent to different departments to be "fixed"; teachers do not always see their role in supporting all needs.	How can we help build a team approach to learning and shared responsibility for the learning of all members of our community?
Parents, teachers, and students are not fully involved in learning support decisions.	How can we build partnerships and bridge the divide between school (within school as well) and home?
We do not have a common language for inclusion.	How can we build a culture of inclusion whose beliefs are reflected in our language and actions?

learned a lot about who we are as a school and many questions were raised about the school we wanted to become.

The team came to three realizations that would help shape our three-step action plan: first, that we needed a guiding vision to carry us forward; second, that we would need time and support for professional inquiry and learning; finally, that we would need to review and revise our systems and structures.

Our Three-Step Action Plan

Step one: Vision setting

We began with our vision for inclusion. It was fortuitous that at the time we were reviewing the needs for learning support, we were also reviewing our school-wide mission statement and learning principles, which helped to shape a shared vision for inclusion that has united all stakeholders. This momentum and the remainder of our three-part action plan are underpinned by three beliefs that serve as guidance to hold us true to our vision of an inclusive school.

Our first belief is that learning is a partnership. Inclusive learning is an integrated partnership between students, parents, staff and stakeholders that provides support in community, in context, and in collaboration for all learners.

> It takes a village to raise a child.
>
> ~ African proverb

Our second belief is that inclusive learning is strength-based. Inclusive learning focuses on the strengths of the individuals and partners in learning in order to break down barriers and enable success for all.

> When a flower doesn't bloom, you fix the environment in which it grows, not the flower.
>
> ~ Alexander Den Heijer

Our third belief is that inclusive learning honors agency. Inclusive learning honors the agency of teachers and students to make decisions and self-advocate for themselves. This has enabled both student and teacher ownership of learning.

> If you want to build a ship, don't drum up the men to gather wood, divide the work and give orders. Instead, teach them to yearn for the vast and endless sea.
> ~ Antoine de Saint-Exupéry

Step two: Professional inquiry and learning

Step two was divided into two phases. First, to build capacity for leadership and second to build capacity for all staff. We began first with the learning of our instructional leaders and learning support teachers so they could help guide the learning of our entire community. Our three beliefs about inclusive learning guided the process of planning for their professional learning.

Our first belief is that learning is a partnership. As a team, we needed to understand how to build partnerships for inclusive education. Members of our leadership team read about teaming and attended conferences and workshops on instructional coaching, co-teaching, and special rights. We then looked at partnerships outside our school. The International School of Bangkok and the New International School of Thailand partnered with us on our journey. We were invited into their schools to learn more about inclusion by sharing their stories and experiences. We also made links to outside agencies in Uganda that could help support and partner with us (e.g., occupational therapists, speech and language specialists, educational psychologists). Through connections with blogs and on social media, we developed a wider professional learning network (PLN).

We then looked at how to better support our leadership to be able to partner with the learning support team. The assistant principal enrolled in the course Learning Diversity and Inclusion from International Baccalaureate (IB, formerly IBO). This course allowed the team to restructure the idea of leadership and bring all voices from our learning community into the strategic planning for inclusion.

Our second belief is that inclusive learning is strength-based. This being so, the instructional leadership team inquired into the ideas of a strength-based approach. We read *Neurodiversity in the Classroom: Strength-Based Strategies to Help Students with Special Needs Succeed in School and Life* by Thomas Armstrong (2012) and organized training based on this for all staff.

Then we made changes to our systems and structures. Our individual education plans (IEP) now start with strengths and we created personal learning profiles, to acknowledge the uniqueness of every learner and celebrate their strengths. Most importantly, we began to really understand what a strength-based school is: one that treats learning diversity as an asset, not a problem.

Our third belief is that inclusive learning honors agency. Thus, the instructional leadership team took time to understand agency in order to support teachers and students to become self-advocates and develop the skills that support lifelong success. The team began researching learner agency through the International Baccalaureate's New Enhanced PYP (IBO 2018). If you choose to come on a similar journey, you might be interested in some of the resources we pulled from for our learning; these are included in our references and resources section below. Please understand we gave ourselves the gifts of time and research to enable our innovation to take place.

After Phase 1, we began to consider how our three beliefs about inclusive learning could guide us in planning for a year-long inquiry into inclusion for our entire learning community. In addition to building capacity to enable inclusion, in Phase 2 we wanted to cultivate agency for all community members and empower innovation in learning.

Our first belief is that learning is a partnership. Thus, we began with partnerships. We shared our vision for inclusion with the whole elementary school staff and asked for their input. Our next step was to begin establishing co-teaching partnerships. We led professional learning sessions on partnering in the inclusive classroom. With this foundation, we started co-planning, co-teaching, and co-assessing to share in the responsibility for all learning. We formed instructional coaching partnerships and built capacity through workshops about differentiation.

Our second belief is that inclusive learning is strength-based. To address this belief in Phase 2, we launched a whole staff book study around strength-based schooling. We began shifting from a deficit approach to learning support to an assets approach to inclusion. We also wanted to extend the strength-based approach to our adult learners. We looked for ways to celebrate the strengths and areas of expertise within our staff. We began by dedicating several of our professional learning sessions to host "Choice Workshops" and "Research and Development Labs," where staff share their learning and understandings with others and showcase the innovative approaches to learning and inclusion taking place in their areas of the school.

Our third belief is that inclusive learning honors agency. As such, we modeled the ideals of an "agentic" (Bandura, 2001) learning community through personal learning journeys (PLJ). Our staff members are encouraged to pursue a passion or interest through an inquiry model. They spend the year interacting with their choice of self-directed learning in partnerships with other staff members. This model for teacher agency has begun to permeate our school culture and is being extended to our students as they have more opportunity for choice, voice, and ownership in their learning by selecting what, where, when, and with whom they learn.

Step three: Systems and structures

The third step in our action plan was to examine the systems and structures that were acting as barriers to inclusion. We set about developing new models for the systems and structures as guided by our three beliefs.

Our first belief is that learning is a partnership. Through our Current Reality Audit, we were led to question: *How can we be creative with the staffing we have to maximize the potential of Learning Support?* We wanted to maximize the expertise of those staff members we already had in place. We restructured the existing department by integrating learning support and English as an additional language teachers as to provide a blended model. We then recruited an extra learning support teacher and reassigned four teaching assistants to be trained more specifically to support the inclusive model of learning. In addition, the position of the counselor was redesigned to be a more integrated role.

Next, we addressed the concept of co-teaching. Each learning support teacher was directly paired with two grade-level teams. This enabled us to allow learning to happen in context as much as possible and removed the idea of learning support being a place to go be "fixed" and instead become a partner in learning.

The final piece to our partnership puzzle was to include parents. We invited parents to share more with us about their child, their passions and strengths, through open-house evenings, conferences, and other school events. We partnered with parents to build capacity through regular weekly Parent Forums and workshops, by publishing detailed grade-level guides and through SeeSaw (online digital portfolios) an interactive tool for sharing learning.

Our second belief is that inclusive learning is strength-based. To address this, we built upon the ideals of coaching. We looked at how we could empower all teachers in their practice for inclusion. We did not choose to have coaches and mentors, but instead developed coaching partnerships based on the strengths of the whole team and the benefit of sharing and supporting each other.

We wanted a community that acknowledges differences as strengths; so each classroom was allocated community time every morning within the schedule, to develop strong bonds that celebrate differences within the homerooms. All student learning should be seen as strengths-based (not just for students with identified needs), so we developed students' Personal Learning Profiles. The purpose was to provide a "one-stop shop" of information about how a student's strengths can be utilized to plan learning to best meet their needs. We used Google Drive to make this accessible to all staff. The profile is populated by students, parents, homeroom teachers, learning support teachers, and all other staff who work with the students, and focus on: students' strengths and identity, strategies that encourage success, and personal goals they have chosen for themselves.

Our third belief is that inclusive learning honors agency. Personal Learning Journeys honor teachers' passions and encourage a sense of engagement and responsibility as a lifelong learner. To honor the agency of our learning community and students we made changes to the structure of conferences and documentation to include more stakeholder voice and ownership, keeping students at the center. Our first conference is a three-way conference where teachers, students, and parents meet to identify strengths and set goals. All voices and opinions are encouraged and valued. Our second conference is a student-led conference, where students decide how they will share their success and learning with their parents and many students communicate this in their home language. Finally, learning support individual education plan meetings and documentation are developed collaboratively with students, homeroom teachers, learning support teachers, and parents. Next, learning support individual education plan meetings and documentation are developed collaboratively with students, homeroom teachers, learning support teachers, and parents. Finally, we looked at how we can offer more opportunities for choice, voice, and ownership in the classrooms. We were inspired by Loris Malaguzzi (1993), who said, "What we want to do is activate within children the desire and will and great pleasure that comes from being the authors of their own learning."

Reflecting on the Journey

Our most important reflection we have come to realize is that inclusion is not something you do, it is something you live. It is not a separate pedagogy for a few. Our three initial beliefs that inclusive learning is a partnership, is strengths-based, and honors agency apply equally to learning for all. In addition to these three beliefs we have expanded our culture of learning to all. We believe that all children are the bearers of important rights and that everyone can learn. We see that the barriers to education lie not within our learners, but within the structures and systems of education and that our strengths will help us overcome our challenges. A successful inclusion journey needs a community commitment, should transcend diversity, and should promote self-advocacy and continually strive to improve. Armed with these new understandings about learning we have some hopes and dreams to continue our inclusion journey.

> Do schools reflect society, or do schools transform society?
> ~ Next Frontier Inclusion (2014)

Innovative Leadership Practices

The innovation in this chapter is about inclusion, but the biggest takeaway from our journey has been about leadership practices: namely, that any institutional change is really about school leaders being culture builders and learning leaders who share the concept of leadership to create a culture of learning that transcends any individual, principal, or leadership team. This leadership enables a school's culture to shift from one of simple compliance of one person's vision to encouraging all staff to develop innovative thinking, which then leads to meaningful ownership of change. Leaders should be humble and accept that they cannot know all the answers. Through respecting expertise and potential both outside and within their own community, leaders can create a culture built on connections and interactions among all members of the school community with shared beliefs and values ensuring that learning will then be driven by all. All members will be learners, encouraged

> to strive for engagement and growth, not perfection, advancing their own ideas and understandings as they find their place in this dynamic world. All members within the culture will then be empowered to share in leadership and act as agents of change to move learning and the community forward into a future we cannot yet imagine—one based in partnerships, focused on strengths, and honoring the agency of all learners.

References

Bandura, A. (2001). Social cognitive theory: An agentic perspective. *Annual Review of Psychology, 52*(1), 1–26.

Hayes, J. D. (2018, October). *Are you ready to make a bold move in your school? Creating modern learning spaces, schedules, and programs to support the contemporary learner*. Plenary presented at IB Global Conference: Shaping our Future in Austria, Vienna.

International Baccalaureate Organization (2018). *Principles into practice: Learning and teaching*. Author: Geneva, Switzerland.

Malaguzzi, L. (1993, June). *Your image of the child: Where teaching begins*. Seminar presented in Italy, Reggio Emilia. Retrieved from https://www.reggioalliance.org/downloads/malaguzzi:ccie:1994.pdf

Pelletier, K., Bartlett, K., Powell, W., & Kusuma-Powell, O. (2014). *The Next Frontier: Inclusion—A Practical Guide for School Leaders*. Retrieved from http://www.nextfrontierinclusion.org/wp-content/uploads/2013/04/NFI-Practical-Guide.pdf

Additional Resources

Authors of Interest

- Anne Beninghof
- Marilyn Friend
- Malcolm Knowles

- Alfie Kohn (https://www.alfiekohn.org/)
- Kath Murdoch (https://www.kathmurdoch.com.au/blog/)
- Sir Ken Robinson
- Bruce L. Smith (writelearning.wordpress.com)
- Carol Ann Tomlinson

Resources of Interest

- Amy Edmondson: *Teaming* (2012)
- Appreciative Inquiry (www.centerforappreciativeinquiry.net)
- Carol Dweck: *Mindset: The New Psychology of Success* (2008)
- Chip and Dan Heath (2010): *Switch: How to Change Things When Change Is Hard*
- Cult of Pedagogy (www.cultofpedagogy.com/)
- Edutopia (https://www.edutopia.org/)
- Harvard Graduate School of Education (HGSE): *Ensuring Success for All: Tools and Practices for Inclusive Schools*
- Harvard Graduate School of Education: *Project Zero* (http://www.pz.harvard.edu/)
- IB Educator Voices (https://ibeducatorvoices.wordpress.com/)
- Jim Knight: Intensive Instructional Coaching Institute with the Instructional Coaching Group
- John Spencer: *Empower: What Happens When Students Own Their Learning* (2017)
- Kevin Bartlett: *Common Ground Collaborative* (https://commongroundcollaborative.org/)
- MindShift KQED (https://www.kqed.org/mindshift)
- Next Frontier Inclusion (NFI)
- Paulo Freire: *Pedagogy of the Oppressed* (1970)
- Reggio Alliance (https://www.reggioalliance.org/)
- Response to Intervention (RTI) (http://www.rtinetwork.org)
- Ross Greene: *The Explosive Child* (1998)
- Simon Sinek: *Start with Why* (2009)

- Study Tours at Reggio Emilia with a focus on special rights (https://www.reggioalliance.org/)
- Tania Lattanzio: *Innovative Global Education*
- Taryn BondClegg (https://makinggoodhumans.wordpress.com/)
- Universal Design for Learning (http://www.cast.org/)
- Yong Zhao: *World Class Learners: Educating Creative and Entrepreneurial Students* (2012)

In Pursuit of International Mindedness

Natasha Haque

Summary

We are living in a time when it is easier than ever to learn about different cultures. Indeed, through migration, people of different faiths and traditions are more likely to live across the street from us, rather than a country away. In international schools, administrators, teachers, and parents celebrate diversity and applaud the way students cooperate peacefully, working together, and celebrate this internationalism. What exactly is being celebrated? The existence of diversity? Globalization? Or something more tangible and definable? This chapter explores the ideas that surround international mindedness and how this can be explored in depth at schools. The chapter also shares the journey of two schools, where curriculum leaders worked with teachers, students, and parents to audit the curriculum and find ways to enhance international mindedness as they defined it for their contexts.

Embracing intercultural understanding is central to the very essence of international education, but it is also increasingly true for schools in non-international settings, especially urban schools, where migration has brought diversity to school populations. However, it is not always a given that just having a diverse student body leads to better intercultural understanding. In this chapter, the strategies used at two schools to explore and develop international mindedness are shared. In both examples, the strategies were led by the curriculum coordinator and supported by the school management leaders. The schools are linked in that I worked at them consecutively and make for interesting comparisons.

The first school was located in Dubai, in the United Arab Emirates. It was established 28 years ago and followed the International Baccalaureate (IB) curriculum. This was a large school with a student body of 2000 students from 82 nationalities but only 2% of the student population was local Emirati. The second school was a 15-year-old IB school located in Dar es Salaam, Tanzania. The school had a much smaller student population of 280 students, 50% of whom were local and the other half a mix of 40 different nationalities. Both schools mentioned promoting international mindedness as part of their mission statements, which were reviewed periodically. It was at these mission statement reviews that questions were asked about what teachers and administrators understood by the phrase "international mindedness." At the end of these meetings and to broaden the discussion, the journey to explore what international mindedness meant at both these schools started with a survey.

Results of the survey from both schools on being internationally minded can be synthesized into three main areas.

1. *Curriculum.* Following an international curriculum (particularly the IB) made parents, students, and teachers feel that the school was promoting international mindedness.
2. *Diverse school community.* Having a diverse school community, particularly many different nationalities, religions, and cultures, promoted international mindedness in not only the taught curriculum but also the hidden curriculum and the culture of the school.
3. *Multilingualism.* Schools promoting multiple languages and mother-tongue maintenance contributed to international mindedness, as speaking multiple languages allowed students to immerse themselves in different cultures.

The results showed that there was a limited consensus on what exactly was meant by international mindedness at both schools. Upon reviewing the survey, the leadership team felt that teachers and students responded generically in a way that diminished a possible deeper meaning. Dissatisfied with the responses, the curriculum coordinator created a tool that looked at how internationally minded the curriculum, pedagogy, assessment, and teachers were at these schools (see Table 6.1). This tool was based on

Table 6.1 Matrix of international minded practices, curriculum, pedagogy, and assessment

	Not Internationally Minded	Economically Driven	Diversity-Driven	Locally Rooted yet Globally Minded
Practices	A school which is not internationally minded and follows an imported curriculum.	An internationally minded school working toward preparing students for a globalized economy.	An internationally minded school focused on diversity.	A locally rooted but globally minded school.
Curriculum	Western curriculum models.	Some recognition of cultural diversity. There is an association that development is related to Western capitalism.	Culturally aware curriculum. Critical curriculum. Multiple perspectives. Social change. Social reflection.	A curriculum that defines and maintains the local culture and recognizes cultural and social differences. Critical curriculum. Multiple perspectives.
Pedagogy	Promote knowledge associated with Western pedagogy.	A focus on teaching English taught to access global markets.	Pedagogy that is pluralistic and in context. English is seen as a transnational language.	Deconstruction of and analysis of a variety of texts and genres representing different cultures (not necessarily originally written in English) to examine social conditions and struggles.

(continued)

Table 6.1 (Cont.)

	Not Internationally Minded	Economically Driven	Diversity-Driven	Locally Rooted yet Globally Minded
Assessment	Western evaluation adapted to local context.	Assessment focuses on the economic advantage and access to the global economy.	Inclusion and an appreciation of a variety of societal roles in different cultures and contexts.	In local language and in cultural and social contexts. Expanding to include complex relationships between multiple identities.
Teachers	Expatriate teachers given privilege over local teachers.	Expatriate teachers with a variety of cultural experience. Proficiency in English.	A mix of teachers offering multiple perspectives and interpretations in a free-flowing curriculum.	Teachers are representative of the community, teaching in a local language and sharing transnational culture, with some expatriate teachers.

work of Wylie (2008, 2011). Wylie created a matrix whereby he considers the theory of what an internationally minded school looks like against the actual practice of international education. His matrix was borne out of his own highly varied experiences of teaching at different international schools, set in different contexts around the world. We took that matrix and personalized it to our context.

Teachers and school administrators at both schools were asked to highlight where they felt the school was in terms of their practices. Interestingly, the administrators in both schools assessed the school as more internationally minded than the teachers did. This tool triggered some deep conversations among both teachers and school leaders.

Some of the key discussion points were:

1. *Reflections on the curriculum.* Interestingly, teachers who were teaching prescribed curriculum for the Diploma Program (DP) exam felt that their curriculum was less internationally minded than their colleagues in the Primary Years Programme (PYP) and Middle Years Programme (MYP). Both programs allow for schools to develop their own culturally sensitive and context-driven curriculum, with teachers creating their units of study. The most heated conversations were about the humanities curriculum. At both schools, historical events such as the First World War were examined through a very Western lens and the subject content was biased toward Western history and philosophy, despite being taught in an Arab or African context. It was realized that a big part of this was driven and maintained by the fact that several teachers in international schools are Western-educated. However, because of these discussions, changes were made to the curriculum that will be discussed later.

2. *Reflections on pedagogy and assessment.* The two schools fell in different sections of the table. In Dubai, teachers felt the pedagogy related strongly with globalization and consumerism. In contrast, the school in Tanzania had more of a critical curriculum, looking at multiple perspectives and social change according to teachers.

3. *Reflections on teacher recruitment.* At both schools, there was a disconnect between administrators' and teachers' perceptions. There was a feeling among some teachers that expatriate teachers

were preferred over local hires and Western education was preferred over Eastern education. This was often driven by parents who could be very vocal, judging teachers on something as superficial as their accent. This impacted the recruitment preferences of the Dubai school, who very clearly advertised for Western-educated expatriate teachers to fill key management positions rather than trying to change perceptions and go for candidates with different educational profiles. It was generally accepted that this is what was wanted in Dubai, and hence an accepted practice. In Dubai, teachers are on two very different types of contracts. First, there are those on expatriate contracts with housing allowances and annual flights back to their home countries. Second, there are those on local contracts with reduced allowances. This left the Eastern and locally trained teachers, who were equally or more competent and sometimes more experienced than their Western colleagues, feeling like second-class employees. Discussions moved to how local faculty and transient expatriate teachers relate and collaborate with each other. At the school in Tanzania, these discussions led to a more proactive policy of creating a balance between local and expatriate staff.

By using this tool and beginning discussions in a safe space, where teachers could share their thoughts in small groups, it became apparent that there were tensions about the content being taught. There were also tensions about how local and international staff related to each other. For example, one of the requirements in the UAE is that Islamic studies are taught to all Muslim students from Year 1 to 13. The teachers of these classes were usually native Arabic speakers and came from a different tradition than the more secular Western expatriate teachers. As a result of this discussion at the Dubai school, the school leaders made a conscious effort to facilitate classroom visits between these groups of teachers to share the different pedagogies they used and break down the stereotypes each group had about the other. Over time, the groupings in the staffroom of teachers also became more mixed.

At the Tanzanian school, the school management decided to appoint an international mindedness champion for the whole school for one year. Using Table 6.1 as a guide, the champion focused on teacher recruitment, curriculum, pedagogy, and assessment. This person periodically surveyed school stakeholders to help assess impacts and changes in perspectives of international mindedness.

Changes in Teacher Recruitment

One of the first outcomes of this championship was a commitment by the school board to recruit both internationally and locally to have Tanzanian staff within every teaching department. To this end, the curriculum coordinator, along with a team of three teachers, developed a free-of-cost teacher training program. Tanzanian teachers from local schools were welcomed to attend weekly seminars on international education and the IB in particular. Teachers who joined the program were invited to shadow classes for nine weeks. Over this period, participants created a portfolio of assignments and reflections on their experiences.

The local curriculum in Tanzania is still associated with significant rote learning and traditional pedagogies. The aim of this program was for expatriate teachers and local teachers to engage with each other and share their experiences and ultimately learn from each other in the pursuit of deeper international mindedness, as well as to train potential local teachers to join the school.

The workshops were fascinating exchanges of ideas and experiences over topics as wide-ranging such as creating authentic units, feedback strategies, summative tasks, art integration, technology integration, resources, and inquiry-based approaches. This process was a powerful conduit to connecting with the wider local community within which this international school is located. Through this activity, we found that there is always a way for international schools to engage with teachers from the local national education scene. Additionally, there is a lot to be gained by bringing the worlds of the local teachers and international school teachers together. For international teachers, it promotes a better understanding of the host country within which they work. It also helps build context rooted in time and place. For local teachers, there is exposure to ideas that they may not have come across and new approaches to try and an awareness of what is happening in international schools.

This program has been running for two years. Participants reported and shared experiences of using what they have learned in their context at their local schools. For the expatriate teachers involved, it has also been a rewarding and eye-opening enterprise and has encouraged them to have a dialogue beyond their immediate communities and challenge some of their preconceived ideas. It also led to several teachers to reflect if we, as international schools, in a non-Western perspective, invest in resource development especially about indigenous knowledge, use resources from homegrown historians, local/regional literature. Since the program has been running, almost all departments within the school have at least one Tanzanian teacher in the team.

Changes to Curriculum

Both in Dubai and in Tanzania, it was realized that the curriculum was influenced by the background and training of the teachers. Schools in Africa and the Middle East offer a rich history and culture, and a great reserve of indigenous knowledge. At both schools, teachers reflected that more could be done to promote authentic curriculum creation and exchange.

For example, within the humanities, the units on the World Wars took a shift to look at the African, Middle Eastern, and Commonwealth contribution to the war efforts. Original units were created and included teachers finding local resources about colonialism and post-colonialism in Tanzania and Africa in general. Our urbanization unit included a rich case study of Dar es Salaam and how the city has grown from its origins as a fishing village to become the colonial capital for first the Germans and then the British, and is now one of the fastest-growing cities in Africa. Similarly, in Dubai students studied how the modern city developed out of a fishing village and trading outpost along the Arabian Gulf. The move away from generic and popular case studies found in textbooks and online resources brought these units alive for students. It was not always easy to find local sources. This is where embracing local colleagues was instrumental in adding richness to our curriculum.

This revamping with a closer reflection on what was being learned goes far in moving away from an imported/adapted curriculum. There is still a need for us as educators to develop mechanisms to share these resources beyond the confines of our schools. To be internationally minded, it should be common to expect students in London or San Francisco to know as much about Jomo Kenyatta and Julius Neyrere as a student in Dar es Salaam or Nairobi knows about Martin Luther King Jr. or John F. Kennedy. Students should encounter literature from different regions. When studying innovations, the contributions of Muslim scholars—such as Ibn Haythem, on whose work modern optics is based, or Al Khawarizmi, the father of algebra—should be included (His Highness the Aga Khan, Prince Karim al Husseini, 2008). By broadening the perspective of the curriculum and resources students are exposed to, they naturally become more internationally minded.

Changes to Classroom Practice

This introspective look at the curriculum led classroom teachers to want to explore and learn more about the heritage and backgrounds of the students in their classes. It became increasingly obvious that to find ways to relate to "otherness," students needed to have a firm grasp of the salient features of their own heritage. One way to make sure that our cultural exchanges moved beyond the superficial was to use an intergenerational personal approach to student research within units of study.

For example, the youngest secondary students in Grade 6 completed a unit on "History of Education." This was a fascinating new unit where students explored how knowledge was passed between different generations, the purpose of schools, and how and who chooses school curricula. They explored how Western and Eastern cultures have historically passed on knowledge over time. Students did their own primary research to discover the similarities and differences between their own, their parents', and their grandparents' school experiences. After interviewing parents and grandparents, students created infographics and were able to see the breadth of experiences the interviews represented. Between all those surveyed, there were 14 countries and 13 different curricular represented. The oldest school experience was a grandparent who went to school in 1936.

The benefits of these activities go far beyond the classroom. Through intergenerational activities, students connected and interacted with different generations within their own families. Students also discovered things they were not aware of, connecting them more securely with their cultural heritage but also making them more aware of the experiences of others. Students were also more engaged, more open-minded, and more interested in the differences and similarities between themselves and their peers. This approach helped students celebrate cultural diversity, embrace different views, and find different ways to relate to "otherness."

 ## Conclusions

Both schools were inevitably influenced by their locations within Africa and the Middle East. The experiences at both schools showed that discussions about international mindedness need to be ongoing so that diverse voices are heard. The idea is working. At a recent Grade 10 celebration assembly, students used the theme of Ubuntu, which encapsulates the African philosophy "I am because we are." Similarly, parents are also contributing different ideas about international mindedness based on their cultures. For example, in one discussion after international mindedness had been a focus at the school for a year, a parent shared a Sanskrit phrase, "Vasudhaiva Kutumbakam," thought to have been written sometime between 500 and 100 CE, which means "The world is a family. One is a relative, the other a stranger, say the small-minded. The entire world is a family, say the magnanimous." Sharing these ideas gives greater depth to discussions around international mindedness, especially in the current zeitgeist.

> ### Innovative Leadership Practices
>
> The biggest innovative strategy was the use of the matrix. It was used to start discussions with teachers and administrators. This tool gave direction to subsequent explorations during unit planning meetings. Another useful strategy was to involve local teachers and bridge the gap between them and expatriate teachers, using the knowledge of local teachers to enrich the curriculum. Finally, the innovation involved bringing multiple perspectives into the curriculum. Ultimately, by keeping discussions around international mindedness alive, these schools were able to engage much more deeply.

> "What is required goes beyond mere tolerance or sympathy or sensitivity—emotions which can often be willed into existence by a generous soul. True cultural sensitivity is something far more rigorous, and even more intellectual than that. It implies a readiness to study and to learn across cultural barriers, an ability to see others as they see themselves. ... The most important reason for us to embrace these new opportunities lies not so much in what we can bring to them as in what we can learn from them."
> —Aga Khan, Prince Karim al Husseini, 2008

References

Aga Khan (2008). Peterson lecture notes. Retrieved from http://www.akdn.org/speech/637/Annual-Meeting-of-the-International-Baccalaureate

Wylie, M. (2008). Internationalising curriculum: Framing theory and practice in schools. *Journal of Research in International Education, 7*(1), 5–19.

Wylie, M. (2011). Global networking and the world of international education. In R. Bates (Ed.), *Schooling internationally: Globalisation, internationalisation and the future for international education* (pp. 21–38). New York, NY: Routledge.

Women in Science: Community Collaboration for Real-World Inquiry

Stephanie Budd and Caleb Steindam

> **Summary**
>
> This chapter describes a middle school Women in Science project conducted in a small international school in West Africa. Students researched historical and present-day gender disparities and conducted interviews with female scientists in their community, publishing a newsletter-style bulletin to share their findings. The project serves as a demonstration of small international schools' capacity for teacher-led innovation and community engagement.

> The first time someone says something [sexist], you shrug it off ... . The second time someone says something, you shrug it off. The 90th time, you stop shrugging it off.
>
> ~ Caroline Simpson (quoted in Jarreau, 2016)

Despite progress in recent decades, women remain underrepresented and underpaid in scientific research and engineering fields. At the Banjul American International School (BAIS), middle school science teacher Stephanie developed an integrated project allowing students to explore this issue inside and outside the classroom.

Context

BAIS is the only internationally accredited school in the small West African country of The Gambia. Student enrollment has fluctuated constantly since BAIS's founding in 1984, ranging from about 20 to 100 students. During the 2017–2018 school year, BAIS had 63 students representing 18 nationalities from Pre-K to Grade 9, and 12 teachers representing 7 nationalities. The school's mission and vision emphasize "embracing diversity" and "valuing integrity." BAIS is committed to developing globally minded and responsible individuals by balancing strong academics with school-wide Character Education and Service Learning programs which are embedded throughout the curriculum.

For this project, BAIS partnered with the Medical Research Council Unit The Gambia at the London School of Hygiene & Tropical Medicine (MRCG at LSHTM), which conducts several research projects in The Gambia while offering training and clinical services in collaboration with the Gambian health system. The main MRCG at LSHTM campus is just down the road from BAIS. Several BAIS students are children of expatriate families who work at MRCG at LSHTM.

International Day of Women and Girls in Science

The BAIS Women in Science Project (WiSP) commenced with an event hosted by MRCG at LSHTM in celebration of the International Day of Women and Girls in Science under the theme "Opening Doors and Closing the Gender Gap." Seventeen schools, including BAIS, participated in this event.

Before walking to MRCG at LSHTM, the BAIS middle school students began the morning with a discussion of biases and struggles described in the article *Being Female in Science* (Jarreau, 2016). Students grappled with their assumptions about equality and opportunity in society as they drew connections to their cultures and lives as well as themes from their humanities classes.

At the event, students learned about MRCG at LSHTM's research projects, training, and clinical services. The theme of the event resonated strongly as students engaged directly with female scientists who displayed passion and enthusiasm in describing their research on the pathophysiology of diet–disease interactions, the ontogeny of immunity, and the epidemiology of diseases in the region. BAIS students recognized and celebrated these women's perseverance and dedication. The event had sparked an eagerness to continue learning.

Background Research

With images of MRCG at LSHTM's female scientists still fresh in their minds, students embarked on deeper analyses of societal and institutional gender disparities in the sciences by examining historical and contemporary statistics. Students self-selected one of four research questions on women's representation in the sciences. Based on their questions, students were assigned partners that they would work with throughout the project. In lessons with the librarian, students applied media literacy skills to find relevant, reliable information sources with statistics represented in graphs, charts, tables, and other formats in line with the Next Generation Science Standards' practice of "Analyzing and Interpreting Data." Students explained the significance of the data, highlighted overall trends, and identified points of comparison across sources. They compared the various ways data were presented and analyzed the purpose and effectiveness of each. Here are some notable facts students highlighted during the activity:

- As of 2016, women accounted for 28.8% of scientific research positions worldwide, and only 18.5% of positions in Southern and Western Africa (UNESCO, 2018).
- Women report raising children, finding child support, and access to mentors as their most significant barriers to working in the sciences (Cell Associates, 2010).
- Opportunities for international travel are integral to career development in the sciences, but pregnancy, breastfeeding, and other family obligations often deter women from pursuing these opportunities (Roca et al., 2018).

After exploring these findings, students were interested in learning how the experiences of MRCG at LSHTM's female scientists compared with the story created by the statistics.

Conducting Interviews

Working in pairs, students researched one of four female scientists working at MRCG at LSHTM, all of whom were mothers of BAIS students. Applying guidelines for professional email etiquette, students developed, revised, and emailed interview requests to the scientists. Drawing on insights and curiosities born from previous stages of the project, each student drafted initial interview questions for the scientists. The class then identified common themes and collaborated to produce one final set of questions in order to achieve consistency and comparability across interviews. Each pair of students emailed the interview questions to their participating scientist.

After receiving the scientists' responses, students participated in a rotating conversation to identify and analyze the similarities in interview data they had received. Students were prompted to think about underlying themes present in the responses and how the responses aligned with the statistics they had gathered.

Women in Science Bulletin

The culminating product was a collaborative newsletter-style bulletin showcasing the lives and work of the four scientists. As a model for their writing, students first read vignettes about influential women in the fields of chemistry or physics from Rachael Ignotofsky's (2016) *Women in Science: 50 Fearless Pioneers Who Changed the World*. Students worked with the librarian to identify attributes related to BAIS's program in character education and discussed how the texts portrayed these attributes through meaningful personal details. Partners were then challenged to capture the essence of their scientist in a one-page profile piece, which encouraged them to apply the scientific writing tenets of conciseness and specificity.

The published bulletin contained an introduction by Stephanie and a profile of each scientist written by the respective student pairs. Students sought to capture the voices and personalities of each scientist by describing life events and illuminating the character traits that helped them succeed in the field. The students designed an original science-themed format for the bulletin with the support of BAIS's information technologies coordinator.

The school director, Caleb, displayed the bulletin at the school entrance and distributed it electronically to all families in the school as an accompaniment to the school newsletter, *The BAIS Buzz*.

Women in Science Luncheon

The culminating WiSP event was a celebratory luncheon. Students collaboratively designed the invitations, which promised the chance to engage in "combustible conversation" with "facts and snacks." Invitees to the event included participating scientists and their families and all middle school students' families and teachers.

Attendees were welcomed to the luncheon with a banner of the periodic table of elements spelling the words "Sc-I-Eu-N-Ce I-S Au-Sm" and a tray of "molecules" made of grapes on toothpicks. Each student spoke briefly, sharing a lesson learned from their scientist. Everyone in attendance rotated in groups through four stations with the following discussion prompts:

- *Why do you feel it is important to instill young scientists, especially females, with a sense of empowerment?* Responses included "re-addressing balance of males to females in the field" and "Because gender unfairness is not discussed as much as it should be. Society is not promoting a positive environment of female scientists."
- *What can we do now to start closing the gender gap in the sciences?* Responses included "increasing the number of role models," "destroying prejudice," and "support and awareness."
- *Why do you think that the sciences are important in our lives?* Responses included "science improves health and understanding of the world around us" and "helps us to improve upon the ways that we do things."
- *What can young scientists do to prepare for a career in science?* Responses included "asking questions," "reading and doing research," and "exploring outside your comfort zone."

Students shared highlights from the conversation and concluded with statements of appreciation for all participants.

 Participant Experiences

After completing the project, participating scientists responded to questionnaires, and students conducted audio-recorded reflections on their WiSP experiences. These responses offer insight into WiSP's impact on participants.

Student reflections

One theme that emerged in several students' reflections was the immense dedication that careers in science require. One student reflected, "I [learned] how hard it is to become a scientist because you have to do a lot of studying." Another commented, "I came to realize that it's quite difficult to become a scientist—not only does it take time, but it takes effort."

Many students demonstrated a deepened understanding of the underrepresentation of women in science. One student commented, "You have to be resilient throughout the whole process ... especially females." Another commented, "It's important to learn about women in science because a while ago, the fields of science were done by men and now more women are in science and more women are encouraged to do science." A third student acknowledged the importance of increasing awareness: "I think the most meaningful thing about this project was the opportunity to help women in science get more attention."

Several students discussed how the scientists demonstrated perseverance and resilience, which were the attributes being emphasized across the school that month for BAIS's character education program. One student commented, "What I learned from [this project] was never give up." Another said, "I learned a lot about perseverance from my scientist and that you have to try and try again until you get what you want." A third expounded more deeply on these themes:

> Going back to character values and how you show resilience ... [the scientist] showed resilience and perseverance throughout her whole process ... not only did people discourage her and she had some rough times, but she was able to push through ... and say, I love this and I feel passionate about science and I feel like women should be able to do whatever they like and what they prefer ... I was so glad that we were able to do this project and see how resilience is put into actual life processes that people go through.

Two female students found the project to be supportive of their ambitions to become scientists in the future. One reflected,

> I think the Women in Science project was important because it showed us that we could be scientists, the girls. We could achieve our dreams ... that there are women doing it and it gave us more confidence towards doing this. ... That was when I really wanted to do astrophysics.

Another female student expressed inspiration in her view that the scientist "felt like she was representing women's rights in that department of science. ... To see that was honestly inspiring towards me because I am thinking in my future to become a chemist." She went on to identify ways that she personalized the scientists' lived experience by saying, "That feeling of accomplishment is something that I too want to feel one day."

Scientist reflections

The participating scientists completed questionnaires about their experiences with WiSP. The scientists identified the most meaningful aspects as "making an impression on young male and female students" and "getting [students] to think about science and the various ways to attain careers in science." One scientist expressed surprise at how much she "enjoyed talking to the students and was keen to listen to their voices and thoughts."

The scientists identified the benefits of carrying out this project in a small school with a close-knit community. One expressed appreciation that "small group discussions were had, interviews were held, which were informative. ... I think that was most meaningful." Another participating scientist stated that "The close interactions with the students may not have been possible in a larger school."

Two participating scientists also shared feedback on the project earlier, during their email responses to the interview questions. One of the scientists commented,

> You probably don't realize, but some of the questions you have asked are quite deep. I have had to think of decisions that I took many years ago. It was a nice exercise. I have tried to explain why I am a scientist, which is a job that I think is very exciting.

Another scientist wrote that she was impressed with the interview questions, which prompted her to ask for further information about the project and its connections to curriculum, remarking in response, "What a thoughtful and interesting project! Thanks for the opportunity of being involved."

Takeaways

The students' reflections demonstrate a heightened awareness of institutional and cultural barriers that women must overcome to succeed as scientists, as well as a heightened appreciation of these women's contributions. Students' enthusiasm was evident throughout the project, especially when they received interview responses, which one student said "felt like Christmas." Two of our female students, who already had aspirations to become scientists, expressed an increased level of passion and motivation toward this goal as a result of the experience.

A notable and unanticipated outcome was that WiSP provided a learning opportunity for the participating scientists from MRCG at LSHTM. The carefully developed interview questions inspired reflection by the participating scientists as they were made to think back over their careers and the decisions that led them to where they are today. The opportunity to share these reflections with young people, some of whom are considering becoming scientists themselves, was a particularly meaningful experience for some of these participants. The scientists all had children at BAIS, so this project enhanced the sense of cohesion within the school community, while also deepening the connections across institutions in the greater community through successful collaboration between BAIS and MRCG at LSHTM.

Discussion

WiSP provided an engaging, authentic learning experience by allowing students to engage directly with experts in the field of medical research. The scientists' enthusiastic participation in this project exemplifies the degree of dedication BAIS families feel for the school and the collaborative relationships the school seeks to cultivate with all members of its community. These relationships develop through regular communication, a welcoming open-door policy for receiving community members' ideas and feedback, and regular invitations for family members to come and share in the students' learning.

Collaborative leadership efforts throughout the school community contributed to WiSP's success. The school director, Caleb, acted as both supervisor and supportive colleague to the science teacher, Stephanie, who designed and coordinated the project. Stephanie, in turn, empowered the students as leaders by giving them authentic decision-making opportunities and putting their voices forward through the published bulletin and the luncheon event. The female scientists from MRCG at LSHTM also served as leaders, taking on mentoring relationships with some of BAIS's young aspiring scientists. Meanwhile, the humanities teacher, the information technology coordinator, and the librarian supported students' work in WiSP as it related to each of their subject areas.

Stephanie demonstrated a great deal of flexibility in the implementation of WiSP without deviating from the project's goals. For example, the initial plan was for students to interview the scientists in person, but the interviews became impossible to schedule with the scientists' travel schedules; the adapted plan to conduct interviews via email achieved the same objectives, while creating opportunities for developing skills for professional email etiquette. Stephanie's adaptable approach allowed for opportunities to incorporate students' ideas into the project, such as the WiSP luncheon which the students planned in collaboration with Stephanie.

WiSP exemplifies how educational innovation can thrive in small international schools like BAIS. Leadership in these schools is shared by necessity; without other administrators to assist with educational programming or supervision, the school head must share responsibilities with the teachers. Communication is frequent and direct, and no bureaucratic layers separate teachers from the school director. Adaptability comes naturally to small international schools like BAIS, which must continually respond to changing conditions in their national, political, and economic contexts. In the previous school year, for example, BAIS had weathered a national political crisis resulting in an unanticipated decrease of more than 25% in student enrollment. Schools that survive and thrive in the face of such challenges grow stronger through them.

Innovative Leadership Practices

It is essential that schools move beyond traditional practices that isolate learning within school walls in order to develop innovative practices that promote learning through real-world interactions. Some of our greatest successes have resulted from opportunities for students to learn from and with members of the school community. Through these interactions, students can make tangible connections between the content of the classroom and the experiences with which they are presented, making the learning more engaging and long-lasting. Every community has valuable experience, knowledge, and expertise. Community asset mapping (Beaulieu, 2002) is a valuable exercise for recognizing the strengths and opportunities within your communities, identifying connections to your curriculum learning goals, and determining ways students can learn from their community. Students will benefit most from these experiences when allowed to have a voice in all aspects of the process, from identifying community assets and connecting with community partners to evaluating and reporting on the learning experience.

Meaningful innovation often occurs when educational leaders provide opportunities for others to lead. Teachers pursue innovation in their teaching when they are taught to view themselves as leaders. Educational leaders must build trust, nurture individual strengths, and encourage risk taking throughout the school. Deliberate efforts should be taken to ensure regular communication among teachers and their supervisors, and to explicitly communicate messages of trust, support, and encouragement for risk taking. When leadership is shared throughout the school, teachers' and students' individual goals are anchored in the school's overall goals, which inspires initiative, creativity, and empowerment.

References

Beaulieu, L. J. (2002). Mapping the assets of your community: A key component for building local capacity. *Southern Rural Development Center*. Retrieved from https://files.eric.ed.gov/fulltext/ED467309.pdf

Cell Associates (2010). *Barriers for women in science survey report*. American Association for the Advancement of Science. Retrieved from https://www.aaas.org/sites/default/files/migrate/uploads/0928loreal_survey_report.pdf

Ignotofsky, R. (2016). *Women in science: 50 fearless pioneers who changed the world*. Berkeley, CA: Ten Speed.

Jarreau, P. G. (2016). Being female in science. *From the Lab Bench*. Retrieved from http://www.fromthelabbench.com/from-the-lab-bench-science-blog/2016/3/8/being-woman

Roca, A., Okomo, U., Usuf, E., Oriero, E. C., Janha, R., Achan, J., & Cerami, C. (2018). African women working in global health: Closing the gender gap in Africa? *Lancet Global Health*, 6(4), 369.

UNESCO (2018). *Women in science*. UNESCO Institute for Statistics. Retrieved from http://uis.unesco.org/en/topic/women-science

SECTION

Curriculum, Teaching, and Student Learning

Introduction to Section III: Curriculum, Teaching, and Student Learning

The core goal of innovations in schools is to ensure that the curriculum is one that supports teaching and learning. This requires a leader who can work across the school to foster a culture of support, innovation, and change. This often requires a leader who is willing to take risks, who is interested in making changes that matter (even hard changes), and who is willing to put students first. Thus, this section highlights innovative practices that directly impact curriculum, teaching, and student learning.

The third section of the book begins with Chapter 8. In this chapter, Jim Gerhard and Gray Macklin discuss how their South Korean school shifted from content-driven to skill-based exams. Jim and Gray lay out the steps that their school engaged in that allowed them to make this paradigmatic shift. Chapter 9 focuses on curriculum structures. In this chapter, Elizabeth Rossini writes about how her school, located in Bangkok, Thailand changed their structures to better align with their philosophy of student learning. This section concludes with a vignette from Daniel Todd. In Chapter 10, Daniel tells the story of Noah, a complex, transnational, multilingual, and anything-but-average student. To better understand the needs of students like Noah (who are not unusual in these highly diverse international schools), his school worked to create personal learning profiles of each and every student.

Innovative leadership practices come to life when discussing the curriculum, teaching, and student learning. For example, shifting the beliefs of how testing *should* be done requires a leader who is comfortable with change, is eager to communicate the innovation, and has a vision for teaching and learning. Additionally, understanding the complexity of third-culture children and being willing to adapt to their learning needs requires a leader who is focused on the socio-emotional well-being of each child. Hence, a vision for leading, teaching, and learning must align with the leader's philosophy of education, as evidenced in their curriculum approach. Innovative leaders thus tend to understand that one of the main roles they play is that of change manager.

Skill-Based Exams: Assessment Promoting the Transfer of Learning Beyond the Classroom

Jim Gerhard and Gray Macklin

Summary

For decades, content-driven final exams have been uncontested assessments that serve as the culmination of all learning over a term of study. Recently, variations on final exams have increased as instructors begin to look for other ways to assess student learning. Because final exams are the culminating assessment for a course, the structure and method of administration can have a transformative impact on the teaching and assessment practices leading up to them. Skill-based activities and exams are a perfect match for the type of preparation students need to demonstrate success in high school and a high degree of preparation for college or university. This chapter shows how the administrators led their traditional school in East Asia away from the content-driven exam to a skill-based exam.

Before getting into how we as administrators led our school in the transition from a traditional system of final exams to skill-based final exams, it is worth looking more carefully at what a skill-based exam is. There are skills involved in every assessment. A skill-based assessment is unique in a couple of key ways.

1. Skill-based assessments target a skill that is considered central to lifelong learning in the content area, even once the student has left a school context.
2. Skill-based assessments eliminate content knowledge or dispositions as potential barriers to demonstrating a skill.
3. Skill-based assessments require repeated practice over time, leading up to the assessment in order to be successful.
4. Skill-based assessments are on-demand, unlike many standards-based assessments that generally collect evidence over time in order to arrive at the performance level of a student.

Skill-based assessment is not the same as standards-based assessment. Standards-based assessment means that student work is evaluated according to broad external criteria or standards. This may be the case as proficiency levels will not be based on a curve, but it is just as likely that a skill-based assessment of specific skills is criterion-referenced.

Identifying the Problem

Because exams are often an unquestioned element of high school, there was very little discontent expressed regarding their administration. Though our leadership team had no difficulty identifying problems with traditional exams, we needed to ask all stakeholders about their concerns so that we were certain to have a comprehensive list and target the right problems for a solution. As we started the shift away from traditional exams, our overarching goal was to arrive at a system that created a unified sense of purpose among stakeholders about what the exams were intended to do and why the change was taking place.

One of the hallmarks of the modern international school is the diversity that often exists not just in its student population, but also in its faculty and administration. While this diversity is an asset for the student experience and professional development, it can pose unique challenges for creating school-wide initiatives requiring a common understanding. Additionally, teachers, students, and parents have existing ideas about assessment rooted not in contemporary academic literature but rather in their own experiences and cultures, and one might be inclined to believe that an assessment culture can never be changed.

Our school is a traditional, highly competitive academic environment. While it was easy for our leadership team to identify the many problems that the traditional exam week created for our school, there was no established alternative that would adequately address issues like scheduling conflicts, seating, and proctoring assignments while also meeting the academic expectations that come with deeply embedded beliefs about the importance of high-stakes exams. As administrators, our preoccupation with logistics resulted in an unwilling acceptance of increased student stress and anxiety, increased incidents of cheating, increased absenteeism, and the loss of valuable instructional time.

The leadership challenge was clear: to devise an exam program that can be administered in the classroom and within the typical class period, that reduced students' dependence on cramming, but did not require teachers to write multiple versions of an exam. We wanted a change that would allow us to spend less time constructing testing schedules and transfer exam time back into classroom instructional time. The solution in our case was the creation of a skill-based exam program; but the shift meant months of intentional work that included curriculum leaders, the school administration, and all faculty.

Before embarking upon a shift in the structure of exams and how they are administered, it was important for us as administrators to establish a clear vision for the primary instructional goals at the school.

Establishing the Goals of Assessment

Collective efficacy, or the shared belief that group action can be taken in order to achieve a specified outcome, is at the top of the list of factors that influence student achievement (Donohoo, Hattie, & Eells, 2018). Because final exams have the potential to impact all instruction leading up to them, the process of moving to skill-based exams creates an ideal set of circumstances for strengthening the sense of collective efficacy in a faculty. The strong academic focus at our school demanded that we establish a strong link between the standards and assessment. We also believed that this shift to an emphasis on skills would have a long-term impact on the level of student engagement in the learning process.

Once our leadership team identified the key problems with traditional exams, we needed to establish a link between the curriculum and how the learning was being assessed. During this process, our whole faculty referred to the learning that students take from a class and apply to unique contexts as *transfer*. Our work with understanding the importance of identifying transfer goals began before we made the decision to change to skill-based exams. By establishing departmental transfer goals, our teachers took a big step toward articulating a larger *why* to students about the learning that was expected of them in a class.

Our faculty members worked to develop a set of between four and eight overarching transfer skills for students to scaffold and navigate each year. This created a clearer picture of priority skills within different content areas. These became guides for the skills to assess in a cumulative exam. These goals created the explicit connection between school curriculum and post-school experiences. For skill-based exams, the answer to the question of why the assessment exists is to determine the likelihood students are progressing toward achieving explicitly stated transfer goals. In our work on skill-based exams, we strove to isolate target skills and evaluate students' proficiency in them.

Prioritizing Standards

As most teachers will tell you, skills are everywhere in their courses. Music and physical education teachers will tell you that skills are 95–99% of what they teach, but teachers in other departments will not be far behind them, especially if asked what they expect students to keep from a class in ten years. As we moved toward skill-based exams, it was important to make sure teachers were identifying the most important skills in their classes so that they could successfully link standards to transfer goals to create exams that evaluated the most important things students were to take with them as they moved on in their academic careers.

It is at this point that a good retinue of likeminded and subject-specific professionals converse about the learning priorities they have for their students, linking them to skill-based outcomes. Fortunately, this was a curriculum focus in our school; so the work we already started doing in one area informed and supported our new direction.

There is an understanding that skills typically come from standards statements. This speaks to the importance of a school having a valid and reliable curriculum. Already actively engaged in curriculum work, our teachers considered students' potential to find success with skill-based exams and design skill development activities because of their proximity to both the curriculum and the students they were teaching. Prioritizing the standards and skills helped teachers to set appropriate targets for assessment and lay out the skills that needed to be introduced, practiced, and then scaled up and refined as the course of study progressed toward the exam. While administrators played a key role in leading this move toward focusing on long-term transfer goals, in the end teacher-led curriculum review and prioritization of standards created an environment where teachers from various backgrounds and beliefs could look at final exams through a different lens.

Planning Instruction

Traditional exams focused primarily on learning content standards. The impact of this focus has been that most instructional time is dedicated to what students should *know* rather than what students should *know how to do*. Understanding this made clear to us what impact the goals of assessment and the priority standards have on how teachers teach. Before the first skill-based exam administration, we had to ensure that teachers were intentionally providing students with learning activities and practice focused on the targeted skills. Ultimately, we wanted teachers to design exams that promoted student confidence, reduced cramming-related anxiety, and maintained high academic standards.

The question is not *if* we should be assessing content knowledge, but rather what other things we should be assessing. There is growing interest in assessing what students will use from their education outside of the traditional classroom. Traditional exams are not adequate for determining the likelihood that transfer will take place. Focusing on skill instruction provides an environment that both contextualizes content learning and promotes the likelihood of transfer beyond the classroom.

For the past five years, we worked to redefine assessment so that it is no longer isolated to tests and quizzes, but rather a complex and ongoing process of interaction between students and teachers. This interaction takes place through the curriculum (i.e., prioritized standards) and its instruction (i.e., learning activities). Instruction that is designed to prepare students to demonstrate skills naturally invites both reinforcing and constructive feedback from teachers along the way, often without the long wait times associated with grading stacks of papers.

During this time, we worked closely with teachers to promote understanding and enthusiasm for the change. Additionally, we made a conscious effort to bridge gaps between teachers within a department or those teaching a course collaboratively. Given the diversity within our faculty, we knew it was unlikely that everyone will be able to seamlessly make the change. How teachers structure their classes is often tied to strongly held personal beliefs and experience that may conflict with this change.

Assessing Targeted Skills

From the outset of the implementation of skill-based exams, teachers and students must know that their goal would ultimately be to demonstrate the skills practiced in a semester. In many ways, this is the ideal situation for education experts who agree that transparency in both *what students should know* and *how students will be evaluated* are central to effective teaching and learning. We wanted our overall academic program to embody this through a clear connection between the instructional activities from the semester and the exam at the end of the semester, but for that to happen we needed exams that challenged students to demonstrate what they know how to do on demand.

Working from transfer skills allowed our teachers to create a vision of where they wanted student learning to be at the end of the semester. Using a backward design approach, our teachers needed to comprehend the complexity of numerous combined skills within a task for a summative assessment. At this point, one of our leadership challenges was the range of ease teachers had designing comprehensive skill-based exams. Parsing out specific skills from standards was a challenge of varying degrees among members of our faculty, but patience and persistent facilitation of collaboration were essential in creating quality assessments.

For example, in the Next Generation Science Standards (NGSS) for biology, some skills students need to master are the ability to evaluate questions, plan and conduct an investigation, and design, evaluate, and refine a solution to a complex real-world problem. Leading up to the exam, a case study might have been an isolated activity in a class, but our teachers and students became much more focused on using class time to work on labs or case studies in order to develop skills that would be intentionally evaluated in the exam.

During the design and review process, we witnessed the evolution exams where students demonstrated skills. In a traditional exam, skills would be marginalized as questions often asked students to choose the correct multiple-choice answer based on a table, diagram, or graph. Because the skill-based exam required students to generate work on their own in class, the exam task was known to all. We were able to move exams from the gym with hundreds of students into their regularly scheduled classes.

A skill-based format is not limited to the sciences. Concise writing, expressing an opinion, validating document information for credibility, and interpreting different perspectives are some of the skills that can be combined as a more complex set of skills targeted for an assessment. Although all these skills are practiced during the semester, a skill-based final shifts them from being a secondary means for accessing content to being the goal of learning itself. By scaling up the skills listed above throughout multiple opportunities in classes, our students worked to master skills that were embedded into learning experiences. We found that having the skill-based exam allowed this type of engagement to occur with teachers and students alike. The thought that goes into the design of an authentic skill-based exam allows all stakeholders to gain the benefits of the method.

Advice for Shifting to Skill-Based Exams

The conversation surrounding a shift from traditional exams is neither top-down nor bottom-up. The shared decision making that supports a successful transition to skill-based exams is an ongoing interaction between administrators, department heads, and teachers. The two key components for us were that the conversation needed to take place over an extended period, not just one or two meetings. It needed to be solution-oriented, where all parties were working toward a common goal. We did this by keeping the administrative focus on the human elements of the change and provided the professionals in their content areas the time and support necessary to identify the skills to be assessed and how they would assess them.

In our competitive international school community, abolishing exams could easily have been read as abolishing rigor and challenge. Moving to skill-based exams freed us from choosing between an assessment strategy that did not support our educational purpose and undermining parents' perception of the quality of education being afforded to their children. In short, we collaboratively developed skill-based exams as a third option when shifting the purpose of final exams.

Up to a year prior, leadership within the school should be developing a timeline for building capacity to complete skill-based exams with students. It is important to note that skill-based assessment questions are a part of any good assessment program and that all teachers typically include such questions on exams. Another note is that most teachers focus appropriately on developing skills across the curriculum that target transfer through their instruction, whether they have consciously chosen to do so or not. By making skill instruction and transfer a school-wide priority, it will be clear that skill-based exams are rooted in both existing teaching practices and the instructional leadership vision. Creating a solid base of effective practice with regards to transfer skills, allowing students to be more actively engaged in both learning and showing what they have learned, and designing exams that allow students to feel a tangible sense of personal accomplishment without the routine stress and worry are all good rationales for helping to sway those reluctant to accept a new approach to final exams.

The two key elements of implementing a new exam format are adequate professional development and a culture of safety where mistakes are acceptable, provided that they are not reflected in student grades. The collective efficacy created from a focus on transfer not only provides a means to view this change systematically, but also allows for much greater professional conversations and sharing of "what really works" in the many unique iterations of international school cultures.

The months leading up to the exams should have built-in times where teachers work on the new exam format. It is important that these times be not mixed in with other meetings or responsibilities but dedicated solely to developing assessments, discussing scoring, and planning practice opportunities for students. Meetings should be varied and focused so that teachers across a department and across the division are in similar places in the process leading up to the exams. It is the administrators' role to effectively allocate and plan a combination of full staff and department meetings as well as workshops and collaborative time for teachers to work with both the curriculum and the assessments themselves.

Ultimately, one of the most important messages we communicated throughout this process was that the school was trying something new and we expected missteps. We established a clear measure of success that allowed room for improvement in subsequent exam administrations. Teachers are rightfully concerned about the accountability mindset of modern education. Knowing the school was prepared to embrace the risk that accompanied the change unleashed considerable creativity. If it is clear that mistakes in the execution of this new approach to exams are not reflected in student grades, there is considerable opportunity not only to learn how to best assess key skills in a class, but also to identify where students are in the development of those skills.

It is important to resist the impulse to make the shift too slowly. Depending on the experience and mindset of the faculty members, the change to skill-based exams is mainly significant from a conceptual standpoint. Assessing skill has always been a part of good exams, but likely never the focus. While some steps in education, demand significant investigation in advance, dragging the decision out for a considerable amount of time will unnecessarily complicate the process.

Following the implementation of a plan, we were careful to reflect on the change with both faculty and students, including how the assessment verified what was learned, as well as what could be done to improve the effectiveness of the implemented plan. Since the first use of skill-based exams at our school was mid-year, there was plenty of time to collect multiple forms of feedback while the experience was fresh. We wanted to know how the different stakeholders evaluated success and what they thought could be done to improve subsequent administrations. Through surveys and conversations with teachers and several focus group sessions with students, we were able to collect feedback that was representative of the opinion of our community.

We found students generally responded positively and reporting lower stress levels, interest in creative assessments, and increased motivation to be engaged in class activities. However, they also noted a lowered sense of accomplishment. Parents were pleased to see their children less stressed, but uneasy with exams students "could not study for."

Teachers generally responded positively to the increased instructional time and reduced time spent on exam logistics, but noted that they would need more time and professional development to improve the quality of skill-based exams.

> ## Innovative Leadership Practices
>
> Innovation and change are often approached in schools with some trepidation. Moving diverse groups of teachers, students, and parents can upset entrenched practices and ideas. Skill-based exams are unique in that they emphasize something universally accepted as essential for students moving into a world where the prevailing constant is change. The conscious assessment of prioritized skills adds weight to skill-focused instruction that has, for too long, been secondary to content-focused instruction. Through the shared experience of curriculum review, standards prioritization, skill-focused instruction, and skill-based assessment, transitioning to skill-based exams have the potential to transform how the stakeholders think about teaching and learning.

Reference

Donohoo, J., Hattie, J., & Eells, R. (2018). The power of collective efficacy. *Educational Leadership, 75*(6), 40–44.

Creating Curriculum Structures That Foster Innovation

Elizabeth Rossini

> **Summary**
>
> This chapter focuses on how schools can develop curricular structures that support creativity, innovation, and choice for students and teachers while directly aligning to the key goals of the school. The philosophy of curriculum development in a school impacts the pedagogy, directly impacting the learning experiences of students. This chapter outlines the curriculum development philosophy and resulting process implemented at International School Bangkok (ISB).

We are educating students born in a very different societal context and living in an era of rapid change. Today's kindergartners will be faced with a very different future when they graduate and join the workforce in the 2030s. At International School Bangkok (ISB), we look at all aspects of our schooling as we attend to the reality of a rapidly changing society. A particular area of interest for us at ISB is: How do we create a curricular structure that supports creativity, allows for innovation, and prepares our international students for roles that we can't even conceive? This chapter is dedicated to answering that question by examining how we, at ISB, are developing curricular structures in ways that keeps our school focused but open for choice and innovation. What we offer is a look at how schools can take the curriculum-related research and global best practice and turn it into actionable change in their buildings. After reviewing our story, educational leaders will gain important insights and learn practical steps to make necessary curricular changes at their school.

ISB is a non-profit organization supporting the learning needs of approximately 1800 students from 66 nationalities with certified faculty from 24 countries. We offer the International Baccalaureate Diploma Program for Grades 11 and 12 and have developed our own international curriculum for grades pre-kindergarten to Grade 10 using curriculum standards from the United States, Canada, Australia, and New Zealand. ISB has been in operation for 67 years and is considered a very established school with a long, successful history within the international community, especially within Southeast Asia.

Responding to Societal Changes

The standards movement in the 1990s brought more alignment between what was expected of learners at a given grade and what was being offered within a standards-based environment. It also brought an often-singular focus on course/grade-level content/skills. At ISB, we are shifting the focus to ensure our students understand the broader ideas and skills within the disciplines that real-world mathematicians, scientists, artists, dancers, language learners, etc. are grappling with. These broad ideas and skills become the conceptual framework for our students to understand the discipline-specific goals that the teacher-designed units/lessons align to.

Our curriculum philosophy has been guided by the seminal work of Grant Wiggins and Jay McTighe (1998) in *Understanding by Design* (UbD). The premise of UbD is twofold. It is, first, to ensure that student understanding, as a goal, is at the forefront of any design work; and second, to ensure quality design practices. Grant and Jay describe the two goals as "the design of curriculums to engage students in exploring and deepening their understanding of important ideas and the design of assessments to reveal the extent of their understandings" (p. 3). Their planning framework asks educators to use a backward design process to be more deliberate about their planning, keeping student understanding at the center of all decisions.

Following on the success of *Understanding by Design*, Wiggins and McTighe (2007) published *Schooling by Design* (SbD), which uses the same process of backward planning to help educational leaders develop mission-driven schools. As teachers are asked to design courses and units with student understanding as the goal, schools should be designing action plans with the mission as the goal. Armed with deep understanding of being a learning-focused school, and driven by our mission, we set out to ensure our curriculum supports these goals. Knowing what to do is often the easier part; making it happen is the challenge.

Freedom Within Structure

Teachers at ISB are instrumental in the development of our challenging, international curriculum. ISB's leadership team believes that authorship is ownership and teachers should be writing, reviewing, and adjusting curriculum in order to provide the most meaningful and responsive learning for their students. This authorship is not blind and without oversight. To ensure we attend to the tenets of SbD and remain a mission-driven school we understand there should be structures in place to support the design of meaningful and engaging learning for our students and have worked hard to put those structures in place. Our curriculum is multifaceted and driven by the broader goals of our school to include ISB's vision and mission, definition of learning, attributes, and values. There is often a belief that the standards are the curriculum, but this is an inaccurate assumption. There are five key areas to ISB's curriculum structure and these are developed for each discipline:

1. Philosophy of learning within the subject area
2. Standards for learning identifying grade-level expectations
3. Macro frameworks identifying broad PK–12, transferable goals for our learners
4. Skills progressions to examine learning across developmental milestones
5. Cornerstone assessments and associated assessment tools

These five components work together to provide the backbone of our macro curriculum and support teachers in developing their course and unit-level curriculum. Our macro curriculum starts with our philosophy statements which identify what we believe about learning in a given subject area.

We use these philosophies to inform our thinking and planning and to shape our pedagogy, and we carefully review and update these to ensure our thinking is current and in line with research. Curriculum standards are another component of our macro curriculum. During a standards adoption process we examine state, national, and international standards to find the best match for our learning needs. If we cannot find ones that meet our stated goals, we write them ourselves.

Macro Curriculum Framework Development and Use

Following the development of subject philosophies and a standards adoption, we then developed macro curriculum frameworks. To do so, we created design teams comprised of 6 to 10 teachers from across PK–12 for one subject area at a time with the purpose of:

- Identifying transferable ideas within and across subjects
- Using these macro frameworks to build coherence across PK–12 and support course/unit development.

The teachers participating in the development of these macro frameworks were recommended by our leadership team and invited to join this work because of their strong curriculum background, their willingness to step outside of the current role to look more broadly at the subject area, and their proven collaborative capacity. This was also a key strategy for developing teacher leaders and supporting their personal growth. Researching and writing macro-level curriculum leads to a deeper understanding of the key learning goals for teachers and ultimately students and becomes an important area of growth for our teacher leaders. These design teams gathered three times during the school year to research and develop the broad learning goals for these macro frameworks. The research involved a deep dive into the subject area and looking at trends, research, curriculum examples, and model frameworks from around the world.

The ISB macro frameworks have three components: (1) long-term transfer goals describing the independent goals we have for our learners; (2) essential questions identifying what we ask our learners to grapple; and (3) enduring understandings describing what we want our learners to understand. The transfer goals, essential questions, and enduring understandings are considered overarching and are written for our most sophisticated learners—our 12th-graders. While these ideas are written with the end in mind, we still want our students across all grades to interact with these ideas as they work toward the same goals. Additionally, these subject-specific macro frameworks have trans-disciplinary goals embedded within, ensuring coherence within and across subjects.

Once the final frameworks were trialed, revised, and finally published, it became an expectation that ISB teachers across PK–12 use the macro frameworks previously described to develop their course and grade-level curriculum, or what we call micro curriculum. Our teachers package their micro curriculum into units of instruction around key learning goals in order to create developmentally appropriate learning for our students just as teachers have always done. The goals from these macro frameworks are built into our curriculum development planner and are easily accessible in drop-down fields. Now our micro (course- and unit-level) curriculum is informed by and aligned with our macro curriculum.

After two years of development, we are now in the middle of implementing these macro frameworks. We are developing more coherence across PK–12 in terms of the big ideas and transferable goals within and across the disciplines and are less reliant on the standards as the only end game. We are embedding these macro frameworks into teaching and learning in multiple ways: first, by aligning our units of instruction to them; second, by using them for cross-grade and cross-curricular collaborations; and third, by coming together in PK–12 groups to examine student learning evidence against these goals.

Aligning our micro curriculum to our macro curriculum

Deliberate alignment between our micro (course- and unit-level) curriculum and macro (PK–12) curriculum facilitates the development of coherence for our teachers and students. Teachers are often assigned to the same course or grade for multiple years and thus have many chances to perfect their teaching for that course or grade. However, students typically have only one year to grasp the learning assigned. As educational leaders, we can ease our students' ability to grasp deep ideas and learn to apply those in their grade-level contexts by ensuring coherence as students move across grades and subjects. A core set of ideas for math, science, music, etc. that are discussed, investigated, and attended to each year provides a coherent lens for our students to attach their learning. These ideas from the macro frameworks become the conceptual lens for students throughout their schooling. Additionally, course- and unit-level designs are much easier to create, as the key learning goals have already been developed and teachers need simply choose the appropriate broad goals for their unit development.

PK–12 subject team meetings

We are also using the macro frameworks to build coherence across grades through biannual meetings in PK–12 subject teams. The teacher leaders who developed the macro curriculum frameworks facilitate these subject meetings to provide time for teachers to focus on student learning needs through a broader lens. Together, the PK–12 teams choose an area from the macro frameworks to focus on, and they bring student learning evidence related to that area. For example, in social studies they examined the essential question of *How can we maintain our values and beliefs while being open to the values and beliefs of others?* For English language arts, they examined the enduring understanding of *Language has the power to clarify thinking, promote connections and influence attitudes and actions.* The teacher feedback from these PK–12 meetings is consistently highly positive. Teachers have expressed how powerful it is to take a central idea from the macro curriculum and look at student learning evidence from our pre-kindergarten learners up to our Grade 12 learners aligned to that goal. As teachers reviewed the 13 years of student learning evidence, they responded to three key questions: *What does the data tell us? What are we doing well? What do we need to work on?* The conversations are rich, steeped in student learning evidence, and aligned with a shared goal. After reviewing the learning evidence, the PK–12 teams celebrate the strengths and discuss and plan for areas for growth.

In the PK–12 science team, they examined the transfer goal of *Conduct investigations, individually and collaboratively, to answer questions.* Through the examination of this goal, the team discovered that our students have a strong understanding of lab-based investigations. The team saw evidence from our youngest learners through our high school learners that they could respond to an investigation, provide a hypothesis, and test their hypothesis using lab-based skills and understandings. However, the examinations of student work revealed that many of the investigations were teacher-directed. The PK–12 discussion regarding the science investigations provided to students revealed that they were not regularly experiencing inquiry-based research. This was tremendous learning for our science teachers, and it has shifted our practice to include more student-driven, inquiry-based research.

Mapping outputs, not just inputs

During the adoption of UbD as our planning framework, we made a key commitment to ground each unit in an assessment of understanding and transfer. In UbD these are called *performance assessment tasks*. As part of backward planning, teachers identify the assessments that will act as evidence of students meeting the learning goals. It is important to recognize that some learning goals are knowledge- and skill-based while others are more complex and require products and/or performances to show understanding. Wiggins and McTighe (1998) identified two key questions to use in the development of performance tasks: What should we look for to find hallmarks of understanding? and What should we look for in determining and distinguishing degrees of understanding? These questions guide the development of a performance task and clear criteria for a given set of learning goals.

At ISB, as part of our micro curriculum development, teachers are required to design assessments of knowledge and skill learning and assessments of understanding and transfer. Being able to break a whole number into parts using fractions is a skill learned in elementary school, which can easily be assessed through traditional means. Being able to use fractions to solve a complex, messy real-life problem requires a different kind of thinking and demonstration. We can use these performance tasks to map the student learning evidence (outputs) that show evidence of our broad goals. Think of teacher written curriculum (course frameworks and units of instruction) as inputs and student-generated work as outputs. It is necessary to have a viable written curriculum, but it is insufficient as the only mapped curriculum. We need also to map and examine what is asked of our students to meet our learning goals—from the standards and also the macro frameworks. Once we have these mapped and attach student learning evidence, we can more easily and routinely examine learning from the student perspective.

We have already mapped our math assessments from kindergarten to Grade 5 and are in the process of mapping the key assessments in Grades 6–10 so we can look longitudinally at our math program and address any gaps or overlaps. If we take this one step further and map those assessments against our macro frameworks and our learner attributes, we can analyze how students are doing on our broad goals, beyond the grade-level standards. If we believe the broad ideas in the macro frameworks are important for our learners, we need to ensure we are helping them achieve them. This additional mapping allows us to examine how we are asking students to transfer their learning and to demonstrate the broad transferable skills that encompass our ISB learner attributes.

Once we complete this kind of mapping (i.e., outputs across grades aligned to the macro frameworks and learner attributes) we can begin to tell stories of what learning looks like at our school. These stories highlight what our learners are doing to show understanding aligned to a key idea. When we combine examples of how students show understanding of the same idea, but across multiple grades, it creates a strong picture of what learning looks like at ISB. These stories highlight how primary learners are grappling with the same sophisticated ideas as our older learners. The stories focus not on the curriculum design from the teacher perspective but rather the learning from the student perspective. Once we capture student-learning evidence attached to these assessments, the stories become even richer and allow us to show learning, through student work across the grades. This is an important next step for us, and one we are working on currently.

One additional way we are using the macro frameworks is through the implementation of program-level assessments. We want to look holistically at student learning evidence across multiple grades to see if the goals of our programs are being met. We are in the process of implementing a cornerstone assessment task in social studies classes focusing on both literacy and social studies skills. The same assessment task is being implemented across Grades 6 through 10, and once these tasks have been completed, we will come together as a social studies team and examine the evidence. The teachers can use the student data at the classroom level, but the purpose is to look holistically at our program and make adjustments accordingly.

In our PK–12 subject team meetings, we look at student learning evidence aligned to the same goal but not from the same task. The focus on the same task context allows us to closely examine a few key goals. Through a collaborative examination of the student learning evidence across multiple grades, we will be able to examine trends in our program and adjust accordingly.

Conclusion

The changes that we made to our curricular structure and practices provided more coherence for both our teachers and students. Grade-level standards are being attended to as necessary, but alongside the broader, more transferable concepts and skills within and across subjects and in concert with the ISB learner attributes. The clarity of our curriculum structure provides our teachers with freedom, within a structure, to create the most engaging and meaningful learning for their students. Our teachers are more empowered to build, generate, and create learning while allowing their students to do the same.

Innovative Leadership Practices

Changing the philosophy of and approach to curriculum development and implementation for a large school is a massive undertaking. Our curriculum development process was a multifaceted, long-term initiative that continues to require many strategic leadership practices.

Anyone thinking about or in the process of shifting an entire curriculum ethos at their school should consider employing the following leadership practices to increase the likelihood of success:

1. *Research and development.* Take time to understand the future context of learning for your students. Meet with many different businesses to understand what they are looking for in current and future employees. Study the future workforce and examine global trends in education and business. Use all of that information to review and adjust what you are doing to prepare students for that kind of future.

2. *Long-range and short-range planning.* Develop long-range plans (three to five years out) that clearly articulate the goals for the initiative and how those goals will be achieved. Include the staffing and budgetary needs as well as the necessary evidence to prove success. Once the long-range plans are approved, develop the short-range annual plans, describing in detail how you will meet the long-range goals.

3. *Develop a communication plan.* Ensure the process and outcome of the initiative are consistently shared with faculty throughout the implementation. Whittle down the plans/goals to a few key ideas that are easily digestible and repeated in all communications. The ultimate goal of ISB's curriculum initiative was twofold: clear coherence across grades and subjects and freedom within structure.

4. *Collaboration.* Build long-term collaborative structures to support the initiative. You will need to return to these structures throughout the implementation.

5. *Develop teacher leaders.* Bring teachers on board as thinkers, developers, testers, and teacher leaders. This team will become a key collaborative structure and an expanded group to help champion the cause of the initiative. Teacher leaders become critical supporters of the work as they test out the ideas in their classrooms.

6. *Change management.* Use a framework to understand, anticipate, and address principles of change theory. Plan for change, review progress toward change, and adjust accordingly.

References

Wiggins, G., & McTighe, J. (1998). *Understanding by design.* Alexandria, VA: Association for the Supervision and Curriculum Development.

Wiggins, G., & McTighe, J. (2007). *Schooling by design.* Alexandria, VA: Association for the Supervision and Curriculum Development.

Vignette: Personal Learning Profiles: Learning for the Unique, Not the Average

Daniel Todd

Summary

This vignette discusses the creation of a system for sharing student learning through Personal Learning Profiles. The author explores the importance of treating every child as a unique learner. He explains how the documentation afforded to students with learning challenges can be applied to all learners through collaboration and shared leadership.

Noah is an average student in an international school. His dad works for USAID and is originally from Virginia in the United States. His mum is a nurse practitioner who works at the United States Embassy; she is originally from Liberia. Noah lived in three different countries since leaving the United States as a three-year-old. His first stay in Mali provided immersion in the French language, and the family has continued to move around the globe with a French-speaking nanny. Noah is an only child and has talents in a variety of areas, mathematics and sciences in particular. Coding and robotics are his passion. He enjoys cross-country and track.

But Noah is not average. The problem with describing a learner as average is twofold. First, as Rose (2014) points out, average learners do not actually exist. Second, the term creates an image of simple solutions. Noah is complex. He speaks three languages: English, French, and Bassa (a dialect of Kru, from his mother's heritage). If you asked his teachers what he struggles with, they would tell you that he finds organizing his ideas difficult and public speaking worries him. He is confident in small-group situations but needs support for larger presentations. His rich linguistic heritage is not something he values. He knows that he can do better with social learning contexts, and with encouragement he could be a strong leader.

This wealth of understanding of Noah's strengths is usually stored in the homeroom teacher's personal memory. At best, it might be shared with a colleague during the grade-level transitions, but most of this rich history of Noah's uniqueness as a learner is never shared. At the International School of Uganda, we changed this practice by taking a leaf out of a few books and writing our vision of each learner.

We were inspired by a Reggio Emilia study tour that focused on children with *special rights* (a term used by Reggio to describe children with learning challenges). The tour taught us that we should not have one pedagogy for children with special rights and another for the neurotypical. At Reggio, there is one pedagogy. So we asked ourselves some "what if" questions. What if everyone had a form of individual education plan? What if every student was listened to and studied, and their needs shared with all their teachers? What if we created a profile of learning for every student?

So we did; we created the Personal Learning Profile (PLP). The PLP is no more than four pages documenting each child's learning history as well as family, cultural, and linguistic background. It includes their learning preferences, strengths, and effective learning strategies.

The first page of the PLP is written by the student and documents their thoughts about their learning, including what learning they enjoy, what their strengths are, and how they learn best. The second page details the child's parental details, family linguistic profile, and other useful demographics. It also includes data about assessment, such as their reading level or other scores. The final page is a short description of the child's strengths as a learner, the challenges they face as a learner, and a list of strategies and tools that have helped to overcome those challenges. The PLP is published as a Google Doc so all teachers can read and edit the document at any time.

The purpose of the PLP is to give every student the opportunity to be understood as a unique learner with personal interests, specific strengths, and challenges. The PLP acts as a catalyst for the idea of relational agency that Prain et al. (2013) discuss how the responsibility for supporting learning is shared teacher–teacher, teacher–student, and student–student. Although the visual-art teacher cannot realistically remember the uniqueness of the 200 children she teaches each week, she can retrieve specific information about specific students she has not completely understood in a PLP database. So after Noah stammered and tore up his paper during an art presentation, the teacher sat down at lunch and retrieved some ideas from the PLP about how to better support Noah in future situations.

At the International School of Uganda, we espouse the belief that the PLP is a simple solution to documenting how each child is a unique and often complex learner. It creates a reference point for all teachers to learn more about the children they are supporting and provides an opportunity for developing their strengths and overcoming barriers to learning. Developing a simple system of documenting the learning profiles and successes of students should not be limited to those with individual education plans; every child deserves to be viewed as neither neurotypical nor typical, and certainly not as average, but as unique.

Innovative Leadership Practices

Through shared leadership, schools can develop a solution for sharing and valuing expertise to build capacity. The enduring value of the PLP is ensured when leadership practices value a multidisciplinary approach to the development of solutions. Therefore, creating a culture of accountability and distributed leadership where colleagues value multiple perspectives while holding each other accountable is a practice any leader can enact.

References

Prain, V., Cox, P., Deed, C., Dorman, J., Edwards, D., & Farrelly, C. et al. (2013). Personalised learning: Lessons to be learnt. *British Educational Research Journal, 39*(4), 1–23. doi: 10.1080/01411926.2012.669747

Rose, T. (2014). *The myth of average: Todd Rose at TEDx Sonoma County* [Video file]. Retrieved from https://www.youtube.com/watch?v=4eBmyttcfU4

SECTION IV

Management of Schools

Introduction to Section IV: Management of Schools

When we think of managing schools, we hardly think "innovation." Yet, in international schools we see innovative things happening around the business of schooling. It may be rethinking how we do things and how those things align with our mission and vision. It may be how we translate research into practice. And it may be how we better align the work that happens in the school with the local contexts. Hence this section is dedicated to understanding innovations in managing schools.

Kim Cofino starts off this section with her chapter on instructional coaching. In Chapter 11, Kim presents three cases that each highlight a different model of instructional coaching. These cases are drawn from her work in China, Singapore, and India. Each exemplifies a different model of instructional coaching. In Chapter 12, Jennifer D. Klein explores how her school adopted problem-based learning, among a handful of other innovative practices. Jennifer lays out a variety of strategies that worked well for her in Columbia. In Chapter 13, John D'Arcy details his work at the Western Academy of Beijing in redesigning the school's learning targets. In Chapter 14, the final chapter of this section, professors Matt Militello and Lynda Tredway detail how they created a doctoral program to address the unique needs of international schools. Matt and Lynda lay out the vision as well as the approach to this innovation.

Managing schools may sound anything but innovative (think numbers and rules and buildings). However, in these international schools, examples of leadership innovation are plentiful. Innovative leaders tend to understand that running a school is about putting learning first and doing that through concerted efforts to empower others and share leadership. This may be done by implementing instructional coaches, shifting to problem-based learning, redesigning the school goals, or even rethinking problems of practices that focus on understanding the intersections of practice and equity. Hence, improving the management of schools requires an intentional communication of the values and intentions, as well as the expected resultant changes.

 # Instructional Coaches: An Investment in Innovation

Kimberly Ann Cofino

Summary

Instructional coaches, particularly in the field of instructional technology, are quite common in international schools in Asia. This chapter highlights different models of coaching as implemented at a selection of international schools. I will explore and compare coaching models at three international schools in Asia. Common strategies include coaching conversations, working with reluctant teachers while empowering enthusiastic teachers, developing and facilitating professional development, and leading school-wide initiatives. School leaders concerned about the cost-to-benefit ratio of hiring coaches will see how the model can lead to positive impact in many areas, ranging from student and professional learning to stakeholder and community buy-in for innovations—making instructional coaching a valuable investment in any school's future.

Introduction

International schools, particularly those in Asia, are fortunate to have the funds, community support, and infrastructure to employ full-time instructional coaches as part of the teaching staff. An instructional coach is a trained teacher whose role is to support teaching and learning through individual, small-group, or whole-school professional development. The primary focus of an instructional coach is individual professional growth for each teacher, which often includes coaching conversations, co-teaching, and modeling instructional practice in the classroom. Instructional coaches are often peer leaders within the school community, especially when they are a content-area expert, like a technology coach or literacy coach. Although some technology instructional coaches do not have teaching responsibilities, many do. This chapter will present case studies of how technology instructional coaches and their roles are currently implemented at three very different international schools: International School Beijing (ISB) in China, United World College Southeast Asia (UWCSEA) in Singapore, and American School Bombay (ASB) in India.

Although these schools implemented different models of coaching, there are some common themes. The models presented in this chapter range from the "traditional" model of instructional coaching at International School of Beijing, to the modified instructional coaching model at United World College of Southeast Asia, to the peer support network of Cognitive Coaching at American School Bombay. The three models demonstrate different levels of development of a coaching program, ranging from full instructional coaching where staffing is provided, to a more peer-to-peer support network with limited staffing. This spectrum can serve as an overview of the different ways that schools can build, enhance, and sustain a coaching culture.

Case Study 1: Full-Time Instructional Coaches at the International School of Beijing, China

The International School of Beijing in China is currently running a traditional coaching model, employing full-time instructional coaches across the school. For those schools with the funds for staffing, this model provides the most formal and structured support for teacher professional growth.

Staffing structures

Only one person on campus has the formal title of Instructional Coach at the International School of Beijing in China, but there are a growing number of teachers who work in a full-time instructional coach role.

These teachers have different titles; however, they work as a K–12 team of coaches across all three divisions of the school, supervised and evaluated by the leadership team in the whole-school Office of Learning. The Office of Learning represents a rather unique hierarchical structure among international schools, where coaches are usually either attached to technology infrastructure, or assigned to specific divisions.

There is one EdTech Facilitator and one Design Facilitator at the elementary level. In addition, the lower elementary school librarian leads technology integration for the younger learners. Similarly, in the secondary school there is one full time MS/HS Design Facilitator and one MS/HS EdTech Facilitator.

The goal of each of these positions is to build capacity and confidence among teachers. Therefore, none of the coaches have a teaching load. Their primary role is to support teachers by planning and facilitating innovative and technology rich learning. With the vision that innovative learning can happen anywhere, there are no technology labs at this school, although there are some dedicated design spaces. There is a push toward design and STEAM in the elementary school and design in the middle school. There are Design Thinking and STEAM labs in each of the three sections of the school (to house the specific equipment needed, like saws and drills) and facilitators lead a lot of the learning that happens in that space, but it is not the facilitator's classroom.

Teacher leaders have all been trained in the Adaptive Schools method, which has created a culture of collaboration across the school. This is a foundational part of building the culture of coaching. The consistency of communication, purpose, and value of collaboration allows all coaches and leaders to use similar language in planning meetings, and to slot right into the rhythm of the meetings and collaboration. These elements of collaboration are now just assumed and part of the language and culture of collaboration at the school.

Benefits and challenges

ISB is in the fortunate position of having a large team of full-time instructional coaches throughout the school. This means the team has a wide variety of skills and interests, and is able to support a wide range of teachers. While they have defined roles, instructional coaches have the flexibility to move between divisions, and act as one team supporting the whole school.

An example of authentic collaboration is when students in the elementary school used the design thinking process in their English as an

Additional Language (EAL) classroom. The EAL and classroom teachers worked with the students to ensure the focus was on language learning, questioning strategies, and designing surveys; while the Design Facilitator supported the high-quality design thinking experience. When asked about their experience, the students noted they weren't preoccupied by the EAL standards because they were so focused on the bigger picture of their learning in context. This engagement and cross-curricular collaboration would likely not have happened without the passionate support and inspiration of the Design Facilitator.

Although having a large team of coaches is an advantage, teachers can easily feel overwhelmed by a large support staff. Unless all instructional coaches are speaking the same language, and working from the same structure, planning meetings can turn into each coach trying to promote their own agenda rather than support the agenda of the team. Another issue is that high-functioning teachers often don't ask for help or share what they're doing with other teachers. Ideally, the instructional coaches at ISB hope that coaching will not be viewed as something only for those who are struggling, but as support for anyone who needs next steps—no matter where they are starting from.

The "traditional" instructional coaching model at ISB is the most formal and structured model of technology instructional coaching profiled in this chapter. This model provides the most consistent model of instructional coaching by employing specific staff members, trained in instructional coaching, to work with all teachers. When building a coaching model or implementing large-scale changes in instructional practice, this model is the one that will allow for most consistency in communication, practice, and structure across divisions or school buildings. Particularly for schools new to coaching, the formal position of an instructional coach can be a huge benefit.

Case Study 2: Technology Mentors at United World College Southeast Asia, Singapore

Each division at this school has a Digital Literacy Coach (DLC). Each works with a small team of teachers called Tech Mentors, who provide peer leadership in the area of technology for learning. This case highlights the specific structure at the middle school level of the East Campus. The structure at the middle school combines "traditional" instructional coaching with a peer-based model to empower teachers to demonstrate leadership within the field of technology for learning. A potential benefit of this model is the ability for tech mentors to reach even more teachers than a single DLC could support.

Staffing structures

DLCs have the primary responsibility of supporting teaching and learning, and at the middle school at East Campus there is another position, that of Tech Mentor. Tech Mentors are teachers who have either been nominated by others or who have applied themselves to be a peer leader within their department for technology. The Tech Mentors system has gradually developed into a strong peer-led technology leadership program providing practical and purposeful professional growth for teams and departments.

Benefits and challenges

The Tech Mentor program recently flourished while focusing on implementing blended learning within each individual mentor's classroom. As mentors, the participants are able to influence culture and change within the school. In this case they have been influential enough that blended learning is now a priority on the strategic plan for the middle school. The combination of a staffed Digital Literacy Coach, along with the support of the leadership team to build a Tech Mentor program, has enabled the middle school to pilot a large-scale blended learning initiative inspired and influenced by classroom teachers. The biggest challenge for DLCs is to prioritize working with Tech Mentors, while balancing their primary job responsibility of working with all teachers.

This case study demonstrates the continued value of a "traditional" instructional coach to lead and facilitate the more peer-driven model of Tech Mentors. This is a clear example of an intermediary step between formal and "traditional" instructional coaching and the full peer-to-peer based model we see in our next case study at ASB.

Case Study 3: Cognitive Coaching at the American School of Bombay

The American School of Bombay has evolved from a "traditional" instructional coaching model, to a peer-based structure where teachers coach each other. For schools where teachers already have a strong understanding of technology for learning and extensive experience with instructional coaching, a peer-based model enables schools to continue to sustain a coaching culture without formal staffing. An additional benefit is the deep understanding of the value and purpose of coaching, because all teachers have been trained.

ASB in Mumbai, India had one of the first 1:1 programs and technology has had a strong presence in the school's plans for learning for over ten years. As the technology integration program developed and teachers became more confident in technology use in the classroom, the school moved away from a full-time instructional coaching model to a peer-to-peer coaching model called Cognitive Coaching. Cognitive Coaching is a series of questioning protocols for fostering reflective conversations in a supportive and nonthreatening way, which anyone can use. These conversations are on an invitational basis and focus on supporting the teacher in recognizing and realizing the solutions they already have within themselves. Because of the peer-to-peer nature of this model, it is easy to grow and sustain a coaching culture as teachers become more competent with the process.

Staffing structures

During the first year of the Cognitive Coaching model, all coaches started their roles without formal training, but were offered in-house professional development. Whenever possible, peer coaches worked within their own department or grade level. After some initial growing pains, the model has changed a bit and the school now works to encourage a peer coach in each year level or department. This allows the peer coaching to be smoothly supported by already existing school scheduling. As the program continues to grow and expand, more and more teachers are applying, and the school is intentionally inviting teachers who would make great peer coaches to apply for the program.

Benefits and challenges

The strengths of this instructional coaching model include how deeply embedded peer coaching is within the school culture. Since each coach is part of a particular team or department, they are essentially a partner in learning. They are always in planning meetings and have a full and deep understanding of the curricular needs as well as the students the teachers are working with. Since they are teachers who are also doing this in the classroom, not an "outside expert" who has a full-time coaching responsibility, coaches are viewed as peers who have professional clout.

In this case study we can see that a history of "traditional" instructional coaching, combined with a well-developed technology-rich learning environment and the budget to train all teachers in the Cognitive Coaching model, allows for a more flexible interpretation of instructional coaching. For schools with a long history of instructional coaching, a deep understanding of the value of coaching, and the time and finances to invest in all-staff training, this model could provide the most sustainable and fully integrated coaching culture.

Essential Elements for Instructional Coaching Success

Although all three schools implemented different styles of instructional coaches, several key commonalities came through both in the interviews and in my personal experience working as a coach in schools in Asia, many of which might prove thought-provoking for anyone interested in innovative leadership practices.

A culture of coaching supports collaboration at all levels

The cornerstone of a quality culture of coaching is strong relationships and trust. When schools invest heavily in staffing for those positions, it often means that leaders also believe in building a welcoming, responsive, and trusting school community. Although the financial investment might initially be in the coaching program (through staffing), the work that is put into making the program successful impacts every corner of the school, from leadership down.

A good example of this is ASB's Cognitive Coaching model, where peer coaches lead all classroom teachers in developing a "Tech Board" of teacher technology mentors to support student voice and choice in the technology they choose. It is the peer coaches who facilitate these conversations and empower teachers to become proactive learners in order to better engage their students.

This and other the other examples above show that innovative leaders should consciously invest effort and resources into fostering a culture of collaboration. This culture of collaboration can prove key not only in the coaching roles, but also simply among teams, teachers, and students. If a coaching culture can support the development of deep and trusting collaboration across all levels and with the support of leadership, the rewards go far beyond the individual or team-based learning experiences that are developed.

Innovation requires advocates

Schools are busy places. In most cases, we tend to have a multitude of initiatives, all requiring the attention and focus of teachers and leaders across the community. In these busy organizations, it is easy for new ideas to get lost or left behind. When innovative school leaders guide a school toward investing in coaches, they are making a commitment to prioritize innovative learning. Although coaches are most likely hired at the teacher level, they become middle leaders in their role as cheerleader, spokesperson, facilitator, and advocate.

We can see this need for school leadership-empowered advocates who then become leaders themselves exemplified at UWCSEA, where Adrienne Michetti, Digital Literacy Coach (DLC), Middle School, East Campus, observed the lack of forward momentum with technology in her division. Specifically because of her unique viewpoint and role within the school, she was able to identify a clear area for growth, and then take action leading to a renewed division-wide focus on blended learning after just one year of focus with her Tech Mentor team.

It is these grassroots, passionate leaders who keep change moving forward among the many competing interests in any school. In speaking to school leaders as part of my research for this chapter, all have mentioned the critical importance of coaches being the vocal advocate for their area of experience, ensuring that it doesn't get lost among all the other responsibilities leaders have on their plate. Without these passionate voices, it is easy to leave behind an initiative that requires substantial change in the structure of teaching and learning.

Change takes time

All of the coaching models explored in this chapter evolved over a number of years. Innovative leadership can require realizing both that change does not happen overnight, and that teachers will need to be guided through this long-term change process by someone with expertise. To ensure that teachers feel both empowered and supported in making those changes, they need someone to walk beside them. Coaches are the change agents at the classroom level.

As described above, ISB illuminates one way to foster long-term innovation. Because they have two instructional coaches for each division, they are able to prioritize innovative learning, in particular Design Thinking and STEAM, to ensure that they are supporting classroom teachers in meeting their goals, as well as moving toward school-wide expectations. Without the advocacy of coaches in their unique positions, it would be easy for those goals to be lost among other competing interests.

School leaders should, therefore, recognize the crucial intermediary role that coaches can play in guiding a sustainable culture of innovation. While every school will have early adopters who are passionate about new ideas, the priority of classroom teachers will always be their classroom and their students, and that this is where coaches come in. For coaches, their students are the teachers. By focusing on the personalized learning of teachers, coaches can ensure that long-term and sustainable change is both practical and achievable in any school setting.

Leadership is key

All of the coaches I spoke with highlighted the critical support their divisional or school-wide leadership provided, both in empowering them and believing in the culture of coaching. Without the support of an innovative and flexible leadership team, coaches are left on their own to define their role, to advocate for their curricular area, and to manage the multitude of demands placed on a non-teaching staff member in a school community.

For example, shifts over time in priority and leadership at ASB have left some questions to be answered. If the currently vacant technology advocacy positions are not filled, it remains to be seen if the peer coaching model will remain as effective as it has been. By contrast, at ISB, where coaches are intentionally located together within the Office of Learning with the support of three administrators in close proximity, it is clear that school leadership is committed to maintaining a focus on coaching's importance to teaching and learning.

While coaching does not "put butts on seats," it fully supports and builds a learning culture that most certainly does. Without vision and advocacy from school leaders, coaches can be left floundering. The focuses of schools ebb and flow, and priorities change over time, but coaching, if supported by forward-thinking leadership, can play a positive role in driving and sustaining innovation in any situation.

Conclusions

It is clear that each implementation of instructional coaching discussed in this chapter is unique to each school community. Taking the time to explore and examine several models in order to ensure that the structures designed for your school community are appropriate will be key to the success of the program. Speaking to school leaders from around the world shows that their advice is consistent:

- Ensure that you have the right person in the role. Personality and interpersonal skills are far more important than technical or curricular skills. Those can be taught over time, but it is much more challenging to change behaviors.
- Empower your coaches to be advocates for their subject area and give them the time, space, and support to act in areas of passion.
- Leverage all facets of your middle-leadership team. For example, encourage collaboration between heads of department, team leaders, and coaches, whereby coaches teach team leaders how to coach, and team leaders teach coaches how to lead.

At the outset, instructional coaches may seem like an expensive investment, but as can be seen in all the above examples, there have been huge growth in professional learning, great strides forward in standards and expectations for teachers, and continued change and innovation over time as new learning opportunities appear. In short, invest in your instructional coaches and they will invest in you and your school.

> ## Innovative Leadership Practices
>
> Innovative leaders recognize the importance of empowering qualified staff to influence change within the school community. Instructional coaching offers a variety of options for grassroots implementation of innovative ideas. Empowering leaders to be advocates for their areas of expertise enables leaders to determine their vision of where the school should go, and then lets middle-level peer leaders like instructional coaches make it happen. The understanding of the power of instructional coaching to move a school forward is key in sustainably implementing innovative practices.

12 Bringing Innovative Practices to Traditional Contexts: Navigating the Challenges of Change

Jennifer D. Klein

Summary

This chapter explores the challenges of shifting Gimnasio Los Caobos, a PK–12 school outside of Bogotá, Colombia, toward student-centered, project-based learning. Caobos is shifting educational paradigms toward purpose-driven, globally connected, relevant student-centered learning to develop next-generation leaders who know their purpose and want to reshape their society. The chapter explores challenges in the school community and social context, addressing change strategies such as using intentional communication, innovative and traditional practices, transformative professional development, strategic partnerships, and student agency to motivate the culture shifts necessary for increasingly innovative practices.

Gimnasio Los Caobos: The School and Its Context

I moved to Bogotá, Colombia in 2017 to lead Gimnasio Los Caobos, or "Caobos," a PK–12 private school serving 600 Colombian children aged 4–18. A project-based school in an educationally traditional and politically divisive region of South America, Caobos faces challenges as we move toward innovative goals some stakeholders struggle to trust. Because Colombian universities base entrance on standardized national exams, the change toward purpose-driven, globally connected, relevant student-centered learning is terrifying for many families. It is clear, however, that such shifts are necessary for countries like Colombia trying to end decades of inequality and war.

Founded in 1991, Gimnasio Los Caobos offers a humanist curriculum in an outdoor learning environment. With a reputation for academic rigor and an emphasis on entrepreneurship, Caobos began its journey toward project-based learning in 2014 to lead educational change and create next-generation leaders who will move Colombia into the future. Efforts included redesigning classroom spaces to remove an artificial "front of the classroom" and create collaborative spaces connected to the outdoor environment; alongside pedagogical shifts that sought to meet academic benchmarks through authentic, project-based experiences.

The divisive political climate in Colombia is challenging for schools implementing progressive education, but the country is also experiencing accelerated change. There is tangible national interest in reconceptualizing the Colombian national identity. However divided the peace process is, it still marks a shift in the development of human talent and the national mindset about which skills our future requires. Colombia needs creative problem solvers who can address challenges and create new industries and opportunities across socioeconomic sectors. Every field requires innovative thinkers and leaders, young people who will disrupt and reinvent ineffective systems, coexist with machines in an increasingly automated world, and create new job opportunities that promote equity and peace for all Colombians.

Preparing students requires replacing "sit and get" education with pedagogies that foster teamwork, problem solving, and self-management. However, most Colombian schools still rely predominantly on traditional instructional strategies, such as lectures, and they assess through exams. Most challenging is a national university system that still relies almost exclusively on grades and standardized national exams for entry.

Furthermore, Caobos is innovating in a context with few pre–service teacher programs focused on innovative education. A project-based education at the highest level requires the transformation not just of instructional practices but of *thinking*: it requires identifying authentic challenges connected to the disciplines, teaching from questioning and student-led inquiry, and trusting students consistently as learners, letting go of the expert mindset of traditional teaching. High teacher turnover in Bogotá makes teacher preparation a constant challenge as we onboard new teachers who, as much as they believe in what we are doing, find it difficult to avoid the teacher-centered practices they were educated with themselves.

Project-Based, Globally Connected, and Purpose-Driven Student-Centered Learning

Adolescent psychologist William Damon (2009) describes young people today as a generation "characterized more by indecision than by motivated reflection, more by confusion than by the pursuit of clear goals, more by ambivalence than by determination" (p. 5). Caobos hopes to combat this challenge through programming designed to help students find their purpose, their *proyecto de vida*. Caobos strives to foster globally minded problem solvers who not only prosper personally through their entrepreneurial enterprises, but who also transform and improve their communities. Ministry of Education requirements are met through relevant, engaging projects that foster skills such as collaboration, communication, critical thinking, and creativity in local and global contexts.

Project challenges and processes mirror the world beyond the schoolhouse and are tied to that world through strategic partnerships and experiences outside the schoolhouse. For example, Caobos students represented Colombia in several international events in 2018, including the International Partnership for Climate Change in Canada, a human rights event in memory of Martin Luther King in France; and the United Nations' Council of Parties (COP-24) in Poland. Because most global challenges are borderless ones that humans must collaborate to solve, we believe intercultural skills such as the ability to honor varied perspectives and priorities are essential to global progress that benefits the largest number of cultures possible, particularly the most vulnerable.

Caobos' founder Felipe Diago embraced the shift to project-based learning (PBL) in 2014: "Those who didn't believe in the importance of the internet, just 20 years ago, and its potential impact on society, believe that we should continue to educate the way we have for more than 100 years. But the abilities and competencies we should cement in these young 'centennials' require a different, progressive education," one which Diago believes must contain elements of traditional education (F. Diago, personal communication, September 27, 2018). In order to foster such competencies, Caobos embraces the design elements and teaching practices of PBL as defined by the Buck Institute for Education (BIE), in combination with the "Stages of Finding a Solution" developed by Ackers and Laur (2017). Rather than marrying one set of innovative strategies, Caobos draws best practices from several educational organizations: the Experiential Learning Network, Project Zero at Harvard, the SCALE Project at Stanford, the Global Online Academy, Modern Learners, and others.

Gabriel Diago (2018), Director of Innovation, envisions Caobos as a "mecca of innovation" like the MIT Media Lab in Boston, "whose purpose is to unite people with different specialties: architects, engineers, musicians, biologists, doctors, lawyers, philosophers, designers, artists, sociologists, psychologists." As Diago told teachers, "there has always been a site where all professions meet in one place. This place is called a school. And that's why a school has the obligation to become a center of innovation with purpose, and this is our reason for existing." Because of this thinking, teachers develop one interdisciplinary project per trimester at every grade level. Leaders would love to break down the division between disciplines eventually, but in the meantime interdisciplinary planning and teaching let students integrate their understandings in ways that mirror the consistently interdisciplinary experience of life beyond the schoolhouse.

Three of our hallmark experiences include entrepreneurship projects in Grades 8, 9, and 10. Following are three exemplars of student products:

1. *A video game that teaches children with developmental challenges to understand the rules of traffic.* Inspired by a younger sibling with Down Syndrome who often ran into traffic, students developed a "serious game" called Mission Street, designed to teach children with disabilities how to walk safely in urban settings. The game won an award from Renault in 2016 in their international Your Ideas Your Initiatives contest.

2. *A petroleum absorption system that cleans up oil spills safely, made of Colombian materials.* Made of 100% organic Colombian hydrocarbons, this student product won the highest prize given at Caobos, and second place in an innovation fair at Universidad de la Sabana in Colombia.

3. *A drone that cleans up plastic chemical land mines in Colombia.* Inspired by a Caobos father working to de-mine Colombia, students developed a drone with chemical sensors, GPS tracking, and photographic capacity to assist in the location and elimination of plastic chemical land mines with less loss of human and animal life.

These products demonstrate the socially conscious entrepreneurial thinking Caobos strives to ignite in every student; each offers a new solution or disrupts old processes for better ones. Each is of benefit not only to those who created the product, but also to the community it is designed to serve.

Change Management in the Colombian Context: Core Strategies

While Caobos is still learning, leaders have identified several core strategies useful for any school trying to innovate in a traditional context. These strategies include the use of intentional communication, transformational professional development, innovative and traditional practices, local and global partnerships, and student voice.

Strategy one: Foster intentional messaging to and constructive involvement of stakeholders

Innovating at Caobos has required thoughtful communication of our vision. Through monthly *Café con la Rectora* events designed as PBL experiences, I engage parents to address driving questions related to their children's education. Cafés invite parents to solve challenges requiring support from home and school, such as increasing students' tolerance for frustration or improving their collaboration skills.

Caobos publishes an educational blog, Revolución Educativa (https://revolucion-educativa.com), where students, educators, and parents share their experiences. We send a monthly newsletter to families, spotlighting student projects and offering educational videos and articles that help parents understand student-centered learning. Caobos is active on social media, where we celebrate student accomplishments and share useful articles. I also write for various national newspapers and magazines, to help shift educational thinking in Colombia and the Spanish-speaking world. Topics have included reinventing the role of teachers, changing the shape of homework, and preparing our students for an automated future.

Perhaps most important is our constructive engagement of parents in the day-to-day life of the school. In 2018, we developed a "School of 600 Teachers," a database of parents and alumni interested in offering their expertise during projects. This database allows teachers and students to connect with parents who have expertise in areas relevant to what students are learning. Parents also remain our most important audience for student exhibitions each trimester, as seeing PBL in action is our strongest argument for its use.

Strategy two: Offer transformative professional development

It is challenging to meet the professional development needs of teachers in a country with few pre-service programs that emphasize innovative education. A few universities focus on student-centered approaches and technology integration, but these programs need time to mature—and require professors skilled in practices they may not have experienced themselves. While many schools "do projects," they are often front-loaded and controlled by teachers, doing little to build students' ability to investigate, problem-solve, and manage their own learning.

In our professional development efforts, we use PBL techniques with the teachers themselves. Instead of front-loading everything teachers need to know, most professional development seeks to foster teachers' skills through inquiry activities and protocols designed to model participant-centered learning. Most of our professional development begins with a driving question focused on an authentic challenge the faculty is facing, pulled from the "need to know" questions teachers have generated. We also offer elective courses based on teachers' passions, to encourage teacher voice and student choice.

Caobos uses teacher portfolios to model authentic learning practices, track professional growth, and encourage continuous reflection. For the past two years, teachers visited three to four colleagues' classes per year, at least one per division, and reflected using BIE's Teaching Practices Rubric. The goal is not to evaluate, but to learn from their colleagues and reflect on their own practices. Teachers also reflect on their own projects using BIE's Project Design Rubric. The leadership team hopes these approaches will help teachers understand the value of reflection, choice, critique and revision cycles, and other facets of participant-centered learning.

Strategy three: Embrace the middle path

One of our biggest lessons is the importance of the middle path. Originally a Buddhist concept, the middle path is not about balance so much as finding middle ground between extremes. As a product of progressive education myself, a graduate of the Open School in Colorado (see Posner, 2009), I believe some traditional teaching and learning belongs inside progressive schools to ensure our graduates thrive in any context, even the most traditional. While we will not compromise our vision, Caobos leaders recognize our context and are building systems that ensure traditional academic success as much as innovative thinking.

Many parents equate children enjoying school with a lack of academic rigor (see Klein, 2018). Guided by their own childhoods, they judge academic quality by the number of tests, quizzes, and right answers produced. Many are challenged by more holistic, skills-oriented project experiences, viewing them as "fluff." Students sometimes go home claiming they've done little in school because they don't perceive the learning involved in activities or protocols designed to help them grow as learners. Teachers who encourage self-management and student-led inquiry are often perceived as "not teaching," and parents sometimes believe teachers should maintain tighter control over students' decisions.

I believe educators should put vigor above rigor and can achieve excellence in traditional measures of academic success through authentic, relevant projects closely aligned to national curricular standards (see Klein, 2016). I agree with John Dewey (as cited in Roth, 2012) that skills will outlive content knowledge and be of more use to our graduates in the long run. And I agree with Paolo Freire (2000) that education is about fostering dialogue and personal conscience, not filling students' heads. Still, Caobos must ensure our students are accepted to the best universities in the country—and that means students must be as successful in traditional, standardized assessments as they are in more authentic evaluations of growth. While we would love to eliminate exams, grades, homework, and academic subjects taught in isolation, using some traditional practices ensures our students can thrive in any context. For example, Caobos closes every trimester with authentic exhibitions of student learning, but many teachers maintain exams in the final weeks as well, particularly in high school, so that students demonstrate their learning in both ways and are prepared for national exams.

To ensure we always function inside the national system as such, Caobos communicates consistently with the Ministry of Education. For example, we were in regular contact with the Ministry when we developed our senior capstone project and senior electives geared toward university studies. These choice-based practices keep seniors motivated and purpose-driven—and having authorization from the Secretary of Education legitimizes our efforts, showing stakeholders that we can meet Ministry requirements and still innovate.

Strategy four: Develop strategic global and local partnerships

Our work relies on local and global partnerships, from classroom experiences to learning opportunities for teachers. Partnerships with local businesspeople help support student growth in our entrepreneurial programs, for example, and all classroom projects are enriched by field trips and expert visits. Developing partnerships with local universities brings PBL to university professors and pre-service teachers. For example, we are partnering in professional development efforts at several universities around Bogotá. Such partnerships help open doors for our students to connect with university experts, ensure that our students' university experiences are more student-centered, and allow us to home-grow teachers for Caobos.

We are developing student teaching and visiting teacher programs, so Caobos will become a laboratory for fostering innovative teachers. However, we also recognize the value of learning from innovative schools around the world. Caobos teachers run classroom partnerships with several schools, including Dalton Academy (China), Colorado Academy (U.S.), and Appleby College (Canada). Caobos is also developing student exchange programs designed to foster global competencies and teach students to innovate and collaborate across the boundaries of culture, language, religion, politics and socio-economic status.

We partner with educational leaders through Caobos' biannual educational conference, the Revolution in Education Congress, which draws innovative thought leaders from around the world for inspiring keynotes and hands-on workshops. Leaders have seen extraordinary growth in Caobos teachers as a result of connecting them with the most important voices in educational change.

Strategy five: Empower student voice in the change process

Even the most controversial change is more acceptable when it comes from students. This is true at Caobos, particularly when we attempt to transform elements of student life traditionally mandated by adults.

The student projects described here were developed as part of the "*Mi Mundo, Mi Pasión*/My World", My Passión senior capstone project, and each has the potential for motivating deep change. In each case, the student recognized a gap or need in our systems on campus, developed an investigation, and presented his/her findings—with specific recommendations for next steps.

1. *Improving the inclusion of students with physical and developmental disabilities.* Nicolás Saldarriaga, a hearing-impaired student, surveyed teachers, parents, and students to measure their readiness for deeper inclusion of differently abled students. His research suggested that while the Caobos community believes in inclusion, not everyone understands what it means to put inclusion into action. The faculty showed the highest disposition for inclusion; interestingly, Nicolás noted that teachers who taught him seemed particularly predisposed to encourage the inclusion of hearing-impaired students.
2. *Improving student leadership systems so leaders can more effectively address challenges in campus life.* Luis Felipe Reyes investigated challenges in student life (i.e., disrespectful behavior among students, weak student services, etc.). Basing his study on the central tenets of Character Counts, Luis Felipe identified a

variety of strategies for improving student leadership to create a more cooperative community culture. He noted that developing cohesion and improving communication among stakeholders was key to well-orchestrated action, and his final report emphasized the importance of clear, concrete, and measurable objectives.

3. *Improving the inclusion of LGBTQ+ students.* In her investigation of LGBTQ+ inclusion at Caobos, Sara Rodriguez found that high school students generally agreed with inclusion and demonstrated respect toward differences in gender and sexual orientation. However, they noted a lack of consistent, natural dialogue with teachers about these topics. Recognizing that lack of knowledge and preparation makes adults uncomfortable with such conversations, Sara recommended training teachers and helping parents become more comfortable with their children discussing gender and sexual identity at school.

4. *Lowering Caobos' impact on the environment through green practices.* David Felipe Gonzales conducted a deep audit of our use of water, plastic, paper, energy and other resources. He also installed an "Ekomuro" with the 5th graders, designed to collect and store water from rain gutters for use in cleaning. His peer, Sofía Santamaria, sold metal water bottles on campus to fund water dispensers which will lower our use of single-use plastics, as well as creating a space and plan for the collection of recyclable materials.

Each of these projects provides a road map for the future of the Caobos community, offering guidance for our continued improvement in the coming years. Because the initiatives come from the minds and hearts of our students, these capstone projects have the potential to create deep, sustainable change in school culture, beginning with the students themselves.

Caobos students will go on to impact local, national, and global progress because they have been raised as problem solvers who know that their voices and innovations matter. At the very least, Gimnasio Los Caobos will be a school students enjoy attending because they are not victims of their own education, but instead experience a community of ownership and purpose that engages and empowers them as learners and leaders.

Innovative Leadership Practices

The strategies described here were designed to address the needs of our conservative, nearly post-conflict context in Colombia, but will serve in any community balancing culturally relevant priorities and innovative practices.

Intentional communication of values, intentions, and vision is key. Constructive parent involvement can also help move any community toward innovation, particularly when there is tension between current and new practices. Transformative professional development for teachers is also central. In order to make training transformative, schools must provide deep, meaningful experiences that are delivered using the target pedagogy.

Leaders in any context must read their community and adapt innovations to suit those realities, finding a middle path that honors history and tradition while encouraging reflection and growth. Strategic local and global partnerships can help enrich the classroom experience and develop teachers' skills. Finally, student voice should be central in any community moving toward innovation. After all, our students will always be our best guides to what they need to make their learning meaningful.

References

Ackers, J., & Laur, D. (2017). *Developing natural curiosity through project-based learning*. New York, NY: Routledge.

Damon, W. (2009). *The path to purpose: How young people find their calling in life*. New York, NY: Free Press.

Diago, G. (2018, August 1). *Opening welcome to faculty*. Gimnasio Los Caobos, Bogotá, Colombia.

Freire, P. (2000). *Pedagogy of the oppressed* (30th anniv. ed.) (M. B. Ramos, Trans.). New York, NY: Continuum.

Klein, J. D. (2018, August 13). Falsos paradigmas: Una buena educación sí puede ser divertida. *El Tiempo*. Retrieved from https://www.eltiempo.

com/vida/educacion/la-educacion-si-puede-ser-divertida-columna-de-jennifer-d-klein-255432

Klein, J. D. (2016, September 11). Language matters in education: Putting vigor over rigor [Blog post]. *Shared World*. Retrieved from http://principledlearning.org/2017/12/28/language-matters-in-education-putting-vigor-over-rigor/

Posner, R. (2009). *Lives of passion, school of hope: How one public school ignites a lifelong love of learning*. Boulder, CO: Sentient.

Roth, M. S. (2012, September 5). Learning as freedom [Editorial]. *New York Times*. Retrieved from www.nytimes.com/2012/09/06/opinion/john-deweys-vision-of-learning-as-freedom.html?r=0

The Future of Learning at the Western Academy of Beijing: A Work in Progress

John D'Arcy

> **Summary**
>
> The Western Academy of Beijing (WAB) engaged all stakeholders in transforming its educational ecosystem. WAB challenged itself to get better at what it was already good at: holistic, child-centered education. For four years WAB has been researching, designing, practicing, and redesigning its educational ecosystem to better meet the learning and developmental needs and interests of every WAB student. As a result, stakeholders generated thousands of ideas synthesized into 21 transformative targets. Conventionally fixed features including schedules, classrooms, curriculum, and the organization of people are being reshaped to be agile and flexible, putting learners at the center of their learning.

Making a Difference

Compelled by its mission to "Connect, Inspire, Challenge: Make a Difference," the Western Academy of Beijing (WAB) began its transformative journey in 2015. By all conventional measures, it is a highly successful, inclusive, learner-centered school. It is a non-profit, pre-kindergarten-to-Grade 12, international school fully accredited by three independent agencies, it serves 1400 children of foreign nationals living in Beijing. WAB's graduates pursue tertiary education around the world with just under half matriculating into North American universities.

Aligned with the Convention on the Rights of the Child, WAB was founded on the belief that all children have the right to an education. For WAB, this means adhering to non-selective enrollment practices and preserving its Mosaic of Diversity (one of the school's five core values). Another core value, Learner Centered, is deeply rooted in the school's beliefs and practices. These two core values are significant drivers of WAB's commitment to providing the finest educational experience possible for every child in its community. WAB's two guiding vision statements for its transformative work are to "more perfectly realize our mission and core values" and "meet the learning and developmental need of every child in our community."

The Future of Learning: FLoW21 Begins

During WAB's 2015 curriculum review cycle it became apparent to the Senior Educational Leadership Team (SELT) that the three components of its curriculum (written, taught, and assessed) were not as aligned to the school's mission and core values as might be expected from a high-performing school. Curious about the possible misalignment of other key systems and structures, SELT questioned whether other features of its educational ecosystem were aligned and purposefully serving the school's mission and core values, or if any had evolved into barriers. To serve this work, SELT identified nine key features of WAB's educational ecosystem: curriculum, teaching and instruction, assessment, schedules and timetables, technology, host country engagement, learner support scaffolds, learning spaces, and professional learning. SELT's inquiries were WAB's first steps toward more authentically living its core values and achieving its mission, leading to more elegantly aligning and purposefully improving these nine features.

Recognizing the interconnectedness of its educational ecosystem features, SELT understood the need to ensure all features remained integrated as they were more elegantly aligned and improved. Embracing WAB's inclusive ethos and understanding the significant work that needed to be done, SELT embraced a whole-community approach to improvement. Guided by WAB's mission and core values, stakeholder groups were invited into the visioning of what the future of learning would be at WAB, with a fundamental goal being genuinely supporting the developmental needs of every student. With the intention of more explicitly and purposefully achieving the school's mission and living its core values, SELT asked its stakeholder groups (students, faculty and staff, parents, administrators, and board members) the following:

> Given what is known about how people learn, about the incredible speed at which the world now shifts, about the changing nature of work, about advanced learning technologies, and if we are genuinely a learner-centered school (one of our five core values), what might the future of learning look like at WAB?

This question was presented to stakeholders during workshops covering issues of character traits WAB should nurture, educational theory, developmental psychology, educational neuroscience, technological disruptions, socioeconomic globalization, and changing global educational paradigms. Each stakeholder group provided insights about what they wanted and expected from the school. Patterns emerged as did marvelous single recommendations. So too did credible reservations. Most significantly, alongside an affirmation of the community's very high regard for the school was an awareness that WAB stakeholders were strongly united in their expectations about what a high-quality, learner-centered education at WAB should include. The following synthesis of parent comments is consistent with beliefs held by all stakeholder groups:

> We want our children to achieve academic success, though not at the expense of their holistic and character development. We want our children to be ethical, passionate, and genuinely engaged in deep, high-quality learning.

The 21 targets

Stakeholders' responses generated thousands of ideas. Patterns emerged, as did a few excellent outlying recommendations. All data points were analyzed, synthesized, and reframed as strategic targets. The targets included big conceptual ideas and practical objectives. Consolidated targets were brought back to representatives of each stakeholder group to be challenged, modified, improved, deleted, or added to. The targets remained flexible as the community conducted research, established and challenged understandings, explored both possibilities and implications inherent in the targets, and learned. After 18 months, the language of various targets was clarified and the number fixed at 21:

1. WAB's culture is learning-focused.
2. WAB develops self-directed learners.
3. Concept-based curriculum.
4. Inquiry-driven learning.
5. Academic and intellectual thinking.
6. All learners are prepared for volatility, uncertainty, complexity, ambiguity.
7. Vertically phased, essential competencies.
8. Competency-based progression.
9. Transdisciplinary, interdisciplinary, and multidisciplinary learning.
10. Co-constructed and personally relevant curriculum.
11. Real-world, connected, practical learning.
12. Individualized schedules/timetables.
13. Individualized instruction and teaching.
14. Vertically and horizontally flexible and variable learner groups.
15. Flexible, diverse and variable spaces.
16. Continuous personalized feedback and reporting.
17. Collaborative teacher planning.
18. Collegial coaching and mentoring.
19. Team teaching.
20. Adaptive support network for all learners.
21. All community members will become ethical and passionate stewards of our community and planet.

To read more details, visit wab.edu/flow21/targets.

Stakeholder feedback about the targets was consistently supportive. However, four targets, though regarded as worthy, raised concerns.

1. *Self-directed learning.* Concerned voices assumed students would function as autonomous agents, without regular and direct adult support. It became necessary to reassure the community

self-directed learning was not replacing direct instruction with free time, reducing teacher support, removing curriculum requirements, or abandoning assessments.
2. *Competency-based progression.* Concerns were shared about students moving too far from their suitable age groupings. Subsequent presentations about how competency-based progression models work lowered concerns.
3. *Co-constructed and personally relevant curriculum.* Stakeholders' worried students would not know what was important to learn, would make inconsequential or non-rigorous curriculum choices, would not complete essential curriculum, and would not be prepared for exit exams. As SELT assured community members the school would not be abandoning its proven curriculum, concerns began abating.
4. *Individualized schedules.* This target garnered the greatest number of red flags. Though stakeholders understood the value of achieving this target, few were able to imagine how it could be realized. Committed to the target, teachers began creating small- and medium-scale opportunities within the normal schedule to give students and themselves opportunities to individualized schedules.

More generally, stakeholders shared concerns about sufficient and timely professional development and teachers' capacity for change while teaching full-time. While many stakeholders were confident WAB students could handle increased agency, others were not convinced. Regarding the transitory experience of the international parent community, concerns were raised about students being able to move back into conventional systems. There was concern that universities were slow to shift admission policies or instructional practices. All concerns continue to inform the development of FLoW21.

Making the change

Having identified nine key features of WAB's educational ecosystem, SELT committed to ensuring their purposeful improvement and alignment. The work to reshape the educational experience at WAB became known as

FLoW21, a creative acronym for "Future of Learning at WAB" and informally referencing the work of Csikszentmihalyi (1990). Initially, the "21" referred to both the year 2021 and the number of targets. But recognizing that the date was overly ambitious and connoted a false sense of product implementation rather than a transformative journey, SELT began connecting the 21 to the number of targets only.

Building on the community's sense of shared ownership, SELT adopted a model of distributed leadership and inclusive decision making. Though this strategy helped the community develop sustainable and widely embraced improvements, a journey as innovative and complex as FLoW21 generates disequilibrium, uncertainty, and both cognitive and affective conflict. To their credit, WAB's board of trustees, senior leaders, teachers, and parents recognize flux and fray as inherent components of genuine learning and improvement both for individuals and organizations. SELT quickly understood that WAB's work fell under the rubric of "complex" rather than "complicated," as described by Larry Cuban (2010). WAB was not implementing an off-the-shelf program with fixed parameters and clear endpoints (complicated). Instead, WAB embraced the messy work of transforming a human organization (complex), characterized by change, conflict, and constant learning.

Three Phase Transformation Plan: A Multi-Year Transformation Journey

WAB began Phase One of its transformation work by reaffirming its mission and core values. Then, stakeholders reflected on beliefs about the purpose of schooling. They described traits they hoped to nurture in every WAB student, and they outlined what the future of learning might look like at WAB. In this phase, teams of teachers and administrators, supported by parent and student representatives, and guided by their vision statements and targets, inquired into how WAB might better serve the learning and developmental needs of every student. Teams took the shape of either committee, working group, or individual action. The different options allowed faculty to select their preferred level of engagement. All of WAB's 200 educators were involved in this team structure. Approximately half joined one of the nine committees and half created their own working groups or individual actions. For two years, teams explored possibilities, crafted possible solutions, and ultimately made recommendations that directly or indirectly moved WAB toward its targets.

The nine committees, one for each of the key educational ecosystem features, were tasked with moving their puzzle piece forward. Each committee was chaired or co-chaired by teachers and supported by at least one SELT member. Committee chairs became Steering Committee members. It was the steering committee that held the work together and moved it forward. The steering committee comprised teachers, SELT, parents, students, and a board member, for a total of 35 people.

At the close of the 2017–2018 academic year, Phase One concluded with a three-day congress where the steering committee consolidated two years of research and ratified recommendations from the teams. More than 80 decisions, ranging from the definition of curriculum (written, taught, and assessed) to the proposed development of six new or improved systems and structures (e.g., progress mentor program) laid the foundations for Phase Two. While many classroom-level decisions were adopted, others required and received approval from the Board of Trustees.

Students and teachers use organizing systems (e.g., instructional strategies) to facilitate learning and teaching within a larger school structures (e.g. curriculum). While they can exercise some agency within conventional system and structures, relatively fixed constructs limit students and teachers from achieving genuine learner-centered education. Phase Two launched in the 2018–2019 academic year and focused community attention on the building of agile and flexible systems and structures needed to support the learning needs of every student. This moved the community from research and inquiry to project development and implementation.

During this phase the steering committee, maintaining representation from all stakeholder groups, continued functioning as an advisory and recommendation body. SELT's role shifted to the management of the major projects, systems, and structures. The board, with final decision-making authority, continued to provide important strategic guidance and financial oversight of FLoW21, which became significant with the design and construction of new learning spaces and the development of technology solutions.

For Phase Two, faculty members joined one of four project groups: *Student Learning*, *Faculty & Staff Learning*, *Community Learning*, or *Learning Systems & Structures*. The four project groups comprised

30 logically associated subgroups. Teachers opted into whichever subgroup most interested them (e.g., math curriculum development, parent learning, professional coaching and mentoring, learning spaces, etc.). Teachers holding positions of responsibility (e.g., department head) were expected to chair a subproject. Chairs reported to a SELT project manager, who in turn reported to the steering committee.

Faculty & Staff Learning and *Community Learning* groups focused on ensuring all stakeholders remained connected and engaged with FLoW21. *Learning Systems & Structures* and *Student Learning* groups established foundations for the development of six essential systems and structures:

- Learning communities
- Learning spaces
- Progress mentor program
- Schedules and timetables
- Technology (learning management system)
- Competency-based curriculum

While several targets will be largely realized when planned systems and structures are in place, others will be achieved only when students, teachers, and school leaders, using new systems and structures over time, transform practices and behaviors to better serve the learning and developmental needs and interests of every student at WAB.

Learning communities

Evolving from conventional classrooms to learning communities in which teams of teachers share responsibility for their students is a paradigm shift. Acknowledging the significant work to be done, in October 2018 SELT began inviting faculty teams, by grade or subject, to undertake this work. Four teaching teams (26 teachers) volunteered; kindergarten, Grade 3, middle school (math, design, and languages), and high school (design, English, humanities, and library).

Adopting a learning communities model enabled WAB to achieve multiple targets. Within their learning communities, teachers will explore the advantages of team teaching (Target 19), flexible student groupings (Target 14), and professional peer coaching and mentoring (Target 18). Students will further develop skills associated with increased agency (Target 2) related specifically to time (Target 12) and space (Target 15).

Learning spaces

Working with the volunteer teams, WAB commissioned the design of four prototype learning spaces each purposely designed for the specific needs of its learning community (early primary, upper primary, middle, and high school). The first two prototypes (middle and high school) were built during the summer of 2019 with the kindergarten and Grade 3 communities scheduled for construction during the summer of 2020. Once proof of concept is established, WAB will proceed with its campus-wide transformation plan.

Underlying the design of all four prototypes spaces are a set of constant principles including the 21 Targets, the Areas of Knowledge and Ways of Knowing (International Baccalaureate, 2019), research about how physical environments activate learning, and research about how learners benefit from diverse learning spaces. The newly designed learning spaces will support the attainment of multiple targets. Though most evident are Targets 15 (flexible, diverse, and variable spaces) and 14 (vertically and horizontally flexible and variable learner groups), the spaces will encourage Targets 2 (self-directed learners), 13 (individualized teaching and instruction), 17 (collaborative teacher planning), and 19 (team teaching).

Schedules and timetables

WAB stakeholders understand that time should be reprioritized as a resource for student learning, rather than the organization of human resources. Using time *for* learning creates important opportunities for individualized pacing through the curriculum. To build capacity and differentiate for the unique needs of individual learners, WAB teachers and students worked with increasingly flexible schedules (Target 12).

Elementary students use self-directed time for both individual and collaborative inquiry as well as core subject learning (Target 2). Middle and high school students have flex time every day and one full day for individualized scheduling (Target 2). As both individuals and the community increase capacity, competence, and confidence with time management, students with demonstrated ability to effectively manage their time will have increased autonomy to do so.

Progress mentor program

As selected conventional systems and structures are replaced or removed, the progress mentor program, a new structure, becomes central to the support and holistic development of students. The program is fundamental to the community's evolution into an adaptive support network for all learners (Target 20). As students become increasingly self-directed (Target 2) and progress through their curriculum, as competencies are attained (Target 8), they are supported by a progress mentor who provides academic, social, and emotional support.

The progress mentor program connects every student with a caring adult in an ongoing relationship. When fully implemented, every student from pre-kindergarten to Grade 12 will participate in a developmentally appropriate version of the program. With access to a digital dashboard of the student's progress, the progress mentor will help students with time management and holistic well-being.

Technology solution

WAB produced a comprehensive functions and features list for its technology solution, needed to support personalized learning and teaching, co-constructed and competency-based curriculum, real-time feedback and reporting, and individualized scheduling. The solution will provide a dashboard of information to each of the key users: students, teachers, mentors, counselors, administrators, and parents. Dashboard information will highlight the growth and progress of each student's holistic development (academic, social, and emotional). Given the very specific requirements of FLoW21 and the need for significant flexibility, finding an off-the-shelf solution proved impossible. WAB is in the process of contracting with a firm to create a customized solution for WAB.

Once the technology is developed, with guidance from their progress mentors and teachers, students will use the dashboard to review academic, social, and emotional progress and create individualized learning plans (Target 2). With their teachers, students will access curriculum and learning experiences, and track their progress through competency-based curriculum (Target 8). As students develop the necessary skills, they will use the system to co-construct their curriculum (Target 10). Teachers will use their dashboards to develop curriculum, schedule instructional sessions (Target 12), create learning experiences, report on student achievement (Target 16), and group students within and across subjects (Target 14).

Competency-based curriculum

Responding to the differing needs of each learner, WAB is redesigning how and when students move through its curriculum. Rather than moving all students through the curriculum at a standardized pace, each student will be afforded greater flexibility regarding the speed with which skills and knowledge are learned (Target 12). The key goal is to ensure students have developed competencies (Target 8) necessary for the next level of curricular complexity before progressing. To this end, WAB faculty are reshaping the curriculum into vertically phased competencies (Target 7). When complete, competencies will be woven into technology-mediated Learning Experiences designed to encourage a diversity of high-quality individual and social learning engagements while allowing for self-directed learning (Target 2) and individualized pacing (Target 12).

Once the six core systems and structures are in place, the community will shift to the next phase. This third phase will afford WAB time to develop expertise with its new systems and structures and address remaining targets. There is no "delivery date" for FLoW21, no end date for phase three. The work will continue until the community has comfortably mastered its transformed self. At that point, WAB will again review its mission and generate a new strategic plan.

Innovative Leadership Practices

Experience suggests that school leaders who claim responsibility for a school's success deny other community members shared ownership. Where ownership is held too tightly by administrators, change initiatives are likely to fail, for two key reasons. First, people who feel ownership of school improvement work assiduously to see it succeed. If ownership is held by leaders, others will be less inclined to dedicate themselves to the work and typically withdraw support when early indicators are less than stellar, which by design is the case for improvement journeys requiring iterative development cycles. Once a critical mass of any constituency group opts to resist an improvement, the chance of sustained success is negligible. Leaders with responsibility for improvement inevitably micromanage faculty, including supporters of the initiative, pushing faculty farther from the work and the leadership team. The second reason improvement initiatives fail is because leaders, regardless of whether they share ownership, leave the school before goal realization, which in the world of international education occurs too often. Improvement initiatives require time, usually more than anticipated, because inevitably they involve changing something about the school's culture and individuals' metal models, which takes years.

References

Cuban, L. (2010, June 8). The difference between "complicated" and "complex" matters. Retrieved from https://larrycuban.wordpress.com/2010/06/08/the-difference-between-complicated-and-complex-matters/

Csikszentmihalyi, M. (1990). *Flow: The psychology of optimal experience.* New York, NY: Harper and Row.

International Baccalaureate (2019). What is the theory of knowledge? Retrieved from https://www.ibo.org/programmes/diploma-programme/curriculum/theory-of-knowledge/what-is-tok/

# A Reimagined Doctoral Program

Matthew Militello and Lynda Tredway

Summary

A reimagined educational doctoral program supports school leaders in international schools to address the equity challenges they are confronting in their contexts. Using innovative curricular, pedagogical, and research methodologies, the Ed.D. program has spearheaded an effort to use participatory action research methodology as a vehicle for equity challenges that crop up in their contexts (see education.ecu.edu/IntEdD). The design elements of the reimagined Ed.D., largely from improvement science and the community learning exchange framework, can be incorporated into similar doctoral programs and into school reform work.

Introduction

Earning a doctorate in educational administration is a journey. Traditionally a challenging journey given that fewer than 40% of the educators who begin the Ed.D. obtain their degrees within seven years of beginning their program. While the research is relatively scant, studies have indicated low estimates of on-time doctoral completion (Most, 2009; Tinto, 1993; Zwick, 1991). Participant attribution is the main focus of low completion and centers on individual variables such as financial and opportunity costs (Bair & Haworth, 2004; Gardner, 2009; Girves & Wemmerus, 1988).

Completing a terminal degree for international educators takes on a special set of circumstances that are not within their locus of control. International school educators have limited access to degree programs based on geographic limitation. More specifically, international educators seeking an Ed.D. or Ph.D. in education most often take online courses and travel abroad for residency requirements. Nonetheless, there has been a press for professional doctorates outside the United States (Bourner, Bowden, & Laing, 2001; Gregory, 1995). The key issues, low completion rate and access to programs for international educators, warrant new programmatic design, including by whom, how, when, and where courses are taught as well as the kind of support that faculty provide students.

The purpose of this chapter is to describe a *reimagined* Ed.D. design *for*, and, in part, *by* international school leaders (see education.ecu.edu/IntEdD). We use "reimagined" to describe our redesign because the process included international school leaders who had completed an Ed.D. program or who were interested in completing their Ed.D. This chapter provides an overview of the program methodology and principles, and then a presentation of the anchor frameworks and structural elements of the reimagined Ed.D. Finally, it details specifics that support program implementation to achieve the goals of access, support, and three-year completion.

The East Carolina University International Ed.D.

Our Ed.D. focuses the entire graduate experience on preparing practitioner researchers who can organize collaborative teams to address issues of equity in their school contexts by collecting and analyzing evidence that supports iterative improvement. Put simply, our reimagined Ed.D. engages international educators in using a single methodology that supports them during and after the program: participatory action research (PAR). The purpose of each Ed.D. dissertation is to improve the practices of international school leaders. The equity focus is informed by the principles of the Carnegie Project on the Educational Doctorate (Perry, 2013), which aimed to differentiate the Ed.D. from the Ph.D. by designing the education doctorate for educational practitioners. The principles have set a standard for programs, like ours, that are seeking to be more learner-centered and focused on developing educators seeking to stay in school or district leadership positions. Thus, the program focuses on six principles (Perry, 2013):

1. Engages leaders to address questions of equity, ethics, and social justice to bring about solutions to complex problems of practice.
2. Prepares leaders who can construct and apply knowledge to make a positive difference in the lives of individuals, families, organizations, and communities.
3. Provides opportunities for candidates to develop and demonstrate collaboration and communication skills to work with diverse communities and to build partnerships.
4. Provides field-based opportunities to analyze problems of practice and use multiple frames to develop meaningful solutions.
5. Is grounded in and develops a professional knowledge base that integrates both practical and research knowledge, that links theory with systematic inquiry.
6. Emphasizes the generation, transformation, and use of professional knowledge and practice.

We found the principles were helpful in designing a program that is attentive to the unique needs of international school educators. Specifically, we focus on the desire for international school educators to merge theory and practice (Principle 5) in order to further develop their practice (Principle 6).

While the Carnegie principles and the Ed.D. programs focused on those principles gathered steam in the United States, little attention was given to using the principles with the international school educator audience. Two additional frameworks anchor the East Carolina University International Ed.D.: *improvement science* and *community learning exchanges*. The frameworks directed our design, pedagogy, engagement with students, participatory action research (dissertation), and most importantly student learning.

Improvement science

Bryk, Gomez, Grunow, and LeMahieu (2015) at the Carnegie Project for the Advancement of Teaching have committed to a school reform effort they term *improvement science*. Improvement science experts say that the human factor for failure is a 6% problem, meaning that only a small percentage of those who seek to improve show results. We found improvement science framework to be useful and accessible to the work of educators in international schools because it supports educators to deeply engage in cycles of inquiry in a familiar context. As a result, they can gather a team of persons to address a focus of practice. International schools have persistent pressures to improve in an increasingly competitive environment. Thus, the framework focuses on metrics of practice and collaboration. Additionally, the improvement sciences led us to design thinking and pedagogical practices in which we engaged students with dynamic and collaborative thinking strategies with these key principles (Bryk, Gomez, Grunow, & LeMahieu, 2015):

1. Make the work problem-specific and user-centered—*What specifically is the problem we are trying to solve?*
2. View variation in performance as core.
3. See the system that produces the current outcomes.
4. Remember this adage: We cannot improve what cannot be measured.
5. Anchor improvements in disciplined inquiry.
6. Accelerate improvement through networked communities.

The improvement science framework became an important feature of our reimagined Ed.D. in coursework and the formation of the dissertation or capstone project. However, we found that we needed to make one component stronger: honoring the context of place and wisdom of people. We were committed to more deeply engaging graduate students in forming communities of practice, termed *networked improvement communities* (NICs) in the Carnegie parlance, and using the funds of knowledge that those communities can bring to reform work (Lave & Wenger, 1991; Moll, Amanti, Neff, & Gonzalez, 1992).

Community learning exchanges

Community Learning Exchanges (CLEs) are built on the fundamental principles that any genuine improvement effort must first honor the context of place and the wisdom of local people. Our program devotes time to investigating place and people in the very context in which students seek to improve. To do so, we embed the CLE axioms in our pedagogy (e.g., gracious space, circles, learning walks, digital stories) as well as our research methodology (i.e., CLE practices offer creative methods for data collection and analyses) (Guajardo, Guajardo, Janson, & Militello, 2016):

1. Learning and leadership are dynamic social processes.
2. Conversations are critical and central pedagogical processes.
3. The people closest to the issues are best situated to address local concerns.
4. Crossing boundaries enriches developmental and educational processes.
5. Hope and change are built on assets and dream of local persons and their communities

The CLE work complemented improvement science in regard to collaborative efforts for improvement. The CLE work became part of the research methodology. Specifically, the PAR project included the integration of *co-practitioner researchers*. The Ed.D. students partner with other constituents that may include educators, parents, students, and/or community members in their context as partners in the improvement effort. As a result, Ed.D. students use a PAR process that includes both local co-researchers and CLE pedagogies to collect and analyze data.

Improvement Science + Community Learning Exchange = Reimagined Ed.D.

Combining the community learning exchange and improvement sciences frameworks addresses the overarching principles of equity and justice to which the program is committed. The community learning exchange framework influenced the improvement of science in three important ways. First, we use the term *focus* of practice instead of *problem* of practice. Second, we ensure that students develop a set of assets as well as challenges or needs that help them diagnose and address their dissertation focus of practice. Third, we have intentionally emphasized the need for inquiry and praxis (action and reflection of Freire, 2000) for each part of the cycle of inquiry, which is termed the *Plan, Do, Study, Act* (PDSA) cycle in the improvement science framework.

More specifically, we merge the two frameworks both in coursework and *intention* (equity focus) and *process* (participatory action research) of each dissertation project. This new, reimagined Ed.D. framework has developed a new normative practice for design and delivery (see Table 14.1). We embrace engaging pedagogies and empower Ed.D. students to work with colleagues in their contexts. Using a participatory action research methodology to improve their practices, the Ed.D. students develop co-practitioner researcher teams at their sites. This team is an integral part of the journey of inquiry and praxis.

Program features

Several program features support the frameworks: length, cohort structure, course sequence, both online and in-person learning, and a different structure for the dissertation that includes context and chapters for each cycle of inquiry.

Program length. The ECU Ed.D. is a three-year program that *includes* three summers of in-person learning and three school years of online learning with completion of a dissertation by spring of the third year.

Cohort structure. Students enter and complete the program as a cohort with a focus on building the ecology of self so that the research practitioners can engage in the ecology of organization (Guajardo, Guajardo, Janson, & Militello, 2016). Students seek to understand their professional and personal selves through the lenses of history, biology, politics, and culture. This work culminates in digital stories shared with fellow students. Then students engage in the iterative work of developing their leader identities in the context of the organization and communities in which they work, culminating in a second digital story after summer three before they complete the dissertation. One of the more important structures is nurturing the cohort network as a support system throughout the program. Peer cohort learning offers a mirror for the learning in their schools with the co-practitioner research groups.

Table 14.1 Reimagined East Carolina University **(ECU)** Ed.D.

Improvement Science Framework	Community Learning Exchange Axioms	ECU Ed.D.
Make the work problem-specific and user-centered.	Conversations are critical and central pedagogical processes.	What is the focus (not problem) of your improvement effort or innovation in your specific context?
View variation in performance as core.	Crossing boundaries enriches developmental and educational processes.	Focus on what works in your specific context.
See the system that produces the current outcomes.		Learn in public: Make your aim/theory of action public and clear.
Remember the adage: We cannot improve what cannot be measured.	Learning and leadership are dynamic social processes.	Develop specific, doable, measurable, and equitable goals: "Soon is not a time and some is not a number." Build those goals and metrics on the iterative and dynamic work of the participants.
Anchor improvements in disciplined inquiry.		Enact the Plan, Do, Study, Act cycle *with* praxis and inquiry—reflective practice.
Accelerate improvement through networked communities.	The people closest to the issues are best situated to address local concerns. Hope and change are built on assets and dream of local persons and their communities.	Honor the wisdom of people and groups to co-generate and collaborate the focus of practice.

Course sequence. The course sequence is designed to increase capacity both in content areas and in research methodology. Students enroll in two courses per semester. The content courses (e.g., Equity and Social Justice or Organizational Theory) engage students in a deeper understanding of practice and the conceptual, theoretical, and empirical literature necessary for broadening and deepening their knowledge of the field of education broadly and preparing them for the rigor of the literature review. In tandem, the research design courses offer a sequenced set of action research methods that provide a blueprint for the thinking about, proposing of, and implementing of a dissertation project with a team of people in their school settings. One key feature that has supported students is a common syllabus for each semester so that the program sequences the learning in ways that fully support and do not overload students, all of whom are working professionals.

Online learning. To date, online environments have typically been interactions like webinars, taped lectures, and asynchronous discussions—mostly what Freire (2000) would term "banking" didactic learning that does not represent how adults learn best (Knowles, 1980). Our challenge was to translate the dialogical learning we value to an online platform so that students could continue to learn from peers, a key component of adult learning that fosters the kind of co-construction and sense-making that we value in classroom learning. We use a mix of online strategies including synchronous webinars and also asynchronous approaches in which pairs and small groups interact. A recent analysis of the online learning in the Ed.D. program indicates that we have been able to achieve a level of engagement and deep learning (Militello, Tredway, & Jones, 2019). As a result, online strategies have regularly brought our international students close together as peer learners.

In-person learning. Regular contact with the instructors is essential for keeping the individuals and the group on track. We have created two annual opportunities for face-to-face meetings with faculty members. First, each summer students attend a learning exchange for two weeks in Bangkok, Thailand. In addition, each cohort member works with a faculty coach. Beyond regular online communication with students, each coach visits each student at the site of their work. The visit during year one has been valuable for the students and for the faculty coach to learn about the context and meet the people and offer advice that is more usable as the faculty coach is familiar with the context in which the graduate student is conducting participatory action research.

Dissertation. All students engage in a PAR project. Students select a focus of practice aimed at improving local practice and outcomes and rooted in an issue of equity. They engage other adults in their context as *co-practitioner researchers*. This methodology, which aligns the principles of the CLE methodologies with improvement science, includes three cycles of inquiry using action research. As a result, students write three findings chapters for each cycle of inquiry. Each chapter is associated with a design course that students take each semester. As a result, the ECU Ed.D. is an eight-chapter dissertation design:

- *Chapter 1.* Focus of Practice
- *Chapter 2.* Focus of Practice Extant Literature
- *Chapter 3.* Context (People & Place) of your Focus of Practice
- *Chapter 4.* Participatory Action Research Design
- *Chapter 5.* Participatory Action Research Cycle I (Categories)
- *Chapter 6.* Participatory Action Research Cycle II (Emergent Themes)
- *Chapter 7.* Participatory Action Research Cycle III (Themes)
- *Chapter 8.* Assertions/Claims and Implications

Innovative Leadership Practices

The dynamic social processes inherent in participatory action research provide an innovation in improvement science by building and sustaining a community of practitioners who can inquire, collect and analyze evidence, and make iterative changes based on attention to the daily qualitative experiences in schools. Our reimagined ECU Ed.D. framework took the technical and useful aspects of the improvement science and added optimism and indigenous ways of knowing and doing to create a philosophy, pedagogy, and research methodology that is meaningful for working doctoral students. The projects have liberated the traditions of research that have been hierarchical and even colonizing (Hunter, Emerald, & Martin, 2013).

Institutional forces have become an issue with reform at all levels of education: *Educators live within institutional structures that remain hierarchical and despite an informed ideology, new information and evidence, and particular focus on equity, the institutional features can effectively squash or limit reform efforts* (Weiss, 1995). Navigating the waters of hierarchy while lifting up the roles of teachers, parents, and students and advocating for more equitable participation in decisions can encounter the institutional pull and one's best efforts can be silenced or thwarted. Our successful, reimagined Ed.D. is a departure from the traditions of innovation in higher education. If such an innovative program can be created in the halls of academia, there is great hope that such reimagined practices can infiltrate K–12 schools.

Innovative K–12 programs and practices require innovative and thoughtful leaders who *live* the CLE axioms *with* their students, teachers, and communities. These leaders can create time and space for conversations across their educational communities. They can practice being more invitational and honoring the context of place and the wisdom of people. Reimagining leadership is not an innovation—it is returning to the ways knowing and improving that have historically proven successful where local relationships deepened through conversations and storytelling. Leaders who engage in this kind of work find allies and are well positioned to hold off the institutional forces and collaboratively implement the innovations our schools and students so richly deserve.

References

Bair, C. R., & Haworth, J. G. (2004). Doctoral student attrition and persistence: A meta-synthesis of research. In J. C. Smart (Ed.), *Higher education: Handbook of theory and research* (Vol. XIX, pp. 481–534). Amsterdam: Kluwer.

Bourner, T., Bowden, R., & Laing, S. (2001). Professional doctorates in England. *Studies in Higher Education, 26*(1), 65–83.

Bryk, A., Gomez, L., Grunow, A., & LeMahieu, P. (2015). *Learning to improve: How America's schools can get better at getting better.* Cambridge, MA: Harvard Education Press.

Freire, P. (2000). *Pedagogy of the oppressed* (30th Anniversary ed.). New York, NY: Continuum.

Gardner, S. (2009). Student and faculty attributions of attrition in high and low-completing doctoral programs in the United States. *Higher Education, 58*(1), 97–112.

Girves, J. E., & Wemmerus, V. (1988). Developing models of graduate student degree progress. *Journal of Higher Education, 59*(2), 163–189.

Gregory, M. (1995). Implications of the introduction of the Doctor of Education Degree in British universities: Can the EdD reach parts the PhD cannot? *The Vocation Aspect of Education, 47*(2), 177–188.

Guajardo, M., Guajardo, F., Janson, C., & Militello, M. (2016). *Reframing community partnerships in education: Uniting the power of place and wisdom of people*. New York, NY: Routledge.

Hunter, L., Emerald, E., & Martin, G. (2013). *Participatory activist research in the globalized world*. New York, NY: Springer.

Knowles, M. S. (1980). *The modern practice of adult education: From pedagogy to andragogy*. Englewood Cliffs, NJ: Cambridge Adult Education.

Lave, J., & Wenger, E. (1991). *Situated learning: Legitimate peripheral participation*. Cambridge, MA: Cambridge University Press.

Militello, M., Tredway, L., & Jones, K. (2019). A reimagined Ed.D.: Participatory, progressive on-line pedagogy. In J. Keengwe (Ed.), *Handbook of research on blended learning pedagogies and professional development in higher education* (pp. 214–242). Hersey, PA: IGI Global.

Moll, L., Amanti, C., Neff, D., & Gonzalez, N. (1992). Funds of knowledge for teaching: Using a qualitative approach to connect homes and classrooms. *Theory into Practice, 31*(2), 131–141.

Most, D. (2009). Patterns of doctoral student degree completion: A longitudinal analysis. *Journal of College Student Retention, 10*(2), 171–190.

Perry, J. (2013). Carnegie project on the education doctorate: The education doctorate—A degree for our time. *Planning and Changing Journal, 44*(3/4), 113–126.

Tinto, V. (1993). *Leaving college: Rethinking the causes and cures of student attrition*. Chicago, IL: University of Chicago Press.

Weiss, C. (1995). The four 'I's' of school reform: How interests, ideology, information and institution affect teachers and principals. *Harvard Educational Review, 5*(4), 571–592.

Zwick, R. (1991). *Differences in graduate school attainment patterns across academic programs and demographic groups*. Princeton, NJ: Educational Testing Service.

SECTION V

Teacher Leadership

Introduction to Section V: Teacher Leadership

Distributed leadership throughout the school is now a regular practice in healthy, well-functioning schools. Leaders who foster teacher leadership understand that these leaders (be it formal or informal) really guide the culture of teaching and learning in their organization. By fostering teacher leaders in school, the international school leaders in this section also foster creativity, empowerment, and lifelong learning.

This section begins with the work of Kristen MacConnell. Kristen focuses Chapter 15 on cultivating teacher leadership at the International School of Nido de Aguilas in Chile. By focusing on distributed leadership, and deeply rethinking her own leadership practices, Kristen offers tangible ways to *hack* leadership. In Chapter 16, Joelle Basnight presents a vignette showing how distributed leadership is evident in student advising. In Chapter 17, Ryan Hopkins-Wilcox discusses how leaders at her school created a culture of learning. Ryan presents how the school shifted away from traditional professional development and towards a professional learning journey where the focus is on finding purpose, making connections, and building a culture of learning. In Chapter 18, Kim Cofino presents a vignette about visiting scholars. In this vignette, Kim writes about how an international school in Japan tapped into the knowledge of experts to translate academic knowledge into practical knowledge through extended on-site visits from experts. In Chapter 19, the doctorate for international teacher leaders is revisited. In this chapter, the authors provide rich details about how the program fosters teacher leadership by confronting equity challenges. Matt Militello and Lynda Tredway co-author this chapter with three of their doctoral students: Tosca Killoran, Christie Powell, and Kristen Halligan. They offer examples of how the program is serving the needs of international schools in China, Singapore, and Thailand.

Innovative leaders know that teacher leadership matters. This being so, leaders highlighted in this section regularly found ways to support this aspect of a learning organization. In this section, we see innovative practices such as creating more actionable meetings through leadership hacks, fostering room for iteration and improvement (and failure), and creating a focus on the learning journey of the individual teacher. Teacher leadership was fostered by bringing in outside experts to serve as visiting scholars to support the work of teachers, hand in hand. This section also offers solid examples of how teacher leaders in international school can serve as translational agents to bridge academics and practice while at the same time serving their unique communities.

Cultivating Teacher Leadership

Kristen L. MacConnell

> **Summary**
>
> This chapter describes one school's journey cultivating teacher leadership. Guided by the driving question "How do we create and facilitate opportunities for teachers to grow in their leadership practices?" the author lays out an approach that begins with developing a deep understanding of the problem and ends with tools and resources that can be adopted by other schools interested in cultivating teacher leadership.

It was 1:15 pm, time for the grade-level team meeting to begin. I walked into an empty classroom. The team leader had a sheepish smile. "I know. They're always late. I sent a reminder. The team should be here soon," she said, her voice trailing off. One of the veteran teachers walked into the room, looked around and said, "I'll be back when everyone gets here." The team leader looked at me, apologized again, and said, "I don't know what to do." The above story is just one example of the types of problems that teacher leaders face when leading a team of their peers.

As someone new to school leadership and as a new faculty member at the International School Nido de Aguilas in Santiago, Chile, I grappled with the best way to support teacher leadership in the Early Years School (EYS) where I was Assistant Director. The EYS has 400 students (50% Chilean and 50% international) and a teaching faculty of 65 (60% Chilean and 40% international). There are six lead teachers and six teaching assistants at each grade level. Teacher leaders are charged with leading 11 of their peers, twice a week, to improve teaching and learning. Facilitating a meeting with 11 colleagues is not an easy task for a skilled leader, let alone a teacher responsible for a full teaching load and limited leadership training.

While this responsibility might be daunting to many teacher leaders, the role of teacher leadership is critically important for improving teaching and learning in schools. When teachers come together to share ideas and strategies about effective teaching practices, learn together from student work, and help each other to solve teaching dilemmas, they make positive impacts on student achievement. Teacher leaders take responsibility for what matters most to them: student learning.

School leaders understand the importance of teacher leadership and the impact it has on teaching and learning. The real challenge for school leaders lies in supporting team leaders and department heads to be effective leaders. Many, if not all, teacher leaders find themselves in leadership roles because they are very effective teachers. However, effective teaching does not equal effective leadership. Von Frank (2011) describes some of these differences as follows: (1) effective teachers reflect on teaching by analyzing and explaining their practice in relation to their classroom, whereas effective leaders are charged with understanding and facilitating instructional change at a systems level; (2) effective teachers are active participants in professional learning communities, whereas effective leaders focus on building the capacity of their colleagues with learning communities; and (3) effective teachers create positive and supportive classroom learning environments by building trust and mutual respect with students to facilitate learning, whereas effective leaders must understand the nuances of adult learning and facilitate and support adults to become better at their craft. It is our responsibility as school leaders to help cultivate the skills necessary for effective teachers to become effective teacher leaders.

While this chapter primarily focuses on the transformation of the team leader meetings in the EYS, I gathered baseline data about teacher leadership from teacher leaders, across all four divisions of Nido de Aguilas (Early Years, Elementary, Middle, and High) to better understand teacher leadership experiences in our school. Through a basic Google survey, I gathered data about formal leadership training, mentoring opportunities, challenges faced by teacher leaders, and factors that helped teacher leaders experience success in their roles. While these data are very specific to Nido de Aguilas, I believe they represent some of the common experiences teacher leaders face in schools.

Survey data revealed that half of the teacher leaders at Nido de Aguilas had little to no leadership training and the other half had taken two or more leadership courses. While I knew we had no formal leadership mentoring at our school for teacher leaders, I was curious whether any informal mentoring was happening. I learned that there were a few pockets of mentoring occurring from current school leadership; however, a large number of our teacher leaders had very limited leadership mentoring at our school or from previous schools.

Teacher leaders reported a wide variety of leadership challenges which included: a lack of purpose for the team's/department's work together, a lack of time to prepare for meetings, being in a leadership role with no real power to make decisions, uncertainty about how to lead difficult conversations, and struggles with the responsibility of holding people accountable for their teaching roles and responsibilities (e.g., having conversations with teachers who skip their recess/lunch duty). Factors that supported teacher leader success included: working with experienced colleagues, the shared belief among colleagues that students' needs come first, feedback from colleagues and school leadership, and a sense of humor.

As a school leader, I rely heavily on teacher leaders to facilitate conversations with teams around the curriculum, teaching practices, and student learning outcomes. Yet many of the teacher leaders struggled to structure these conversations in meaningful ways. Each had the content knowledge to lead conversations about teaching and learning, but struggled with the procedural knowledge to effectively lead change with their peers. In addition to gaps in procedural knowledge, some faced cultural and age differences that contributed to their leadership challenges.

Why Is Distributed Leadership Important?

The concept of distributed or shared leadership is gaining traction in schools. International schools have teaching faculty with a wide range of expertise. Having structures in place to leverage that expertise generates opportunities for capacity building and school improvement (Harris, 2014). When international schools leverage teacher expertise and cultivate the leadership skills necessary to lead change, our schools will become more dynamic institutions of teaching and learning.

Building capacity for teacher leadership in international schools is important because teacher leaders often remain in their teaching positions at a school longer than school leaders. As principals and assistant principals come and go, there can be significant impacts on student learning unless the school has strong systems for curriculum leadership in place. Moving toward a model of shared leadership between school leaders and teacher leaders helps guarantee a viable curriculum. When international schools establish structures for cultivating and sharing leadership, responsibility for student learning is collective as opposed to falling on the shoulders of one to two key people.

What Are the Conditions for Teacher Leadership?

I wondered how we could create conditions and facilitate opportunities for teachers to grow in their leadership practices in meaningful ways within our system. An idea was born. What if we rethought the existing structure of our team leader meetings? What if instead of funneling information from school leadership to team leaders to teachers through our team leader meetings, we ran leadership seminars in which we modeled effective leadership strategies for our teacher leaders to learn, practice, and implement in their own team meetings? As a school leader, I attended grade-level team meetings each week. Participation in these meetings would allow me to provide feedback to team leaders about their meeting facilitation. At our team leader meetings, the team leaders could reflect on how the facilitation moves worked in their grade level team meetings and receive additional feedback and suggestions from each other. This idea led to a transformation in our practice. Our team leader meetings changed from 45-minute biweekly informational meetings to leadership seminars where new skills were learned and leadership challenges were discussed. I used cycles of continuous improvement to learn which structures and conditions yielded actual improvements in teacher leadership.

From Team Leader Meetings to Leadership Seminars: Transforming the Process

I had a better understanding of the types of challenges our team leaders faced, but I needed specific data to plan meaningful leadership seminars. To deepen my understanding of the problem, I interviewed the team leaders and asked them to identify their strengths as a team leader, the specific challenges they faced leading their team, and some areas they wanted to develop further as a leader. Teacher leaders asked questions like "Who needs to be in our meetings?", "How do we hear everyone's voice with so many team members?", "How do we get everything accomplished in such a short amount of time?", and "How do I empower my team members to share their ideas so it doesn't feel like I am the only one who is talking in the meeting?"

Mapping a Plan Forward

In our first seminar, we developed a problem statement being that "Our teams lack a clear purpose, engaged members, accountability, and are not maximizing the expertise and knowledge of our colleagues." Then we brainstormed all of the different factors contributing to this problem. We looked at our list of contributing factors, clustered similar ideas together and created categories from these ideas. In some cases, the name for these categories was obvious to everyone. In other cases, we needed further discussion to dial down from a broad category of a problem to a root cause. To do this, we asked a chain of "Whys." This type of questioning helped us develop a deep, shared understanding of what we meant by the different categories contributing to our problem.

The main issues contributing to our problem were: lack of knowledge about effective leadership strategies, lack of a meeting process, lack of a common goal or a shared purpose, time, communication, cultural differences, lack of meeting norms, general dysfunction (i.e., "general lameness" was the word the teachers settled on), people in survival mode (i.e., a need to keep your head down and just do your work), and lack of support/modeling/mentoring from school leadership. Once we identified all of our categories of problems, we engaged in a process to help identify which of these categories were causes of the problem and which categories were just effects. Often in school we jump to brainstorming solutions to problems without understanding if our solutions are addressing a cause or an effect. If our solutions address effects, our ideas don't work, or they only work for a short period, leading to further frustration.

Theory of Action

I set a goal to guide our learning seminars: "By June 2018, our teams will have a clear purpose and engaged members, will hold each other accountable for planning and running learning-centered meetings, and will maximize the knowledge and expertise of our colleagues to improve teaching and learning." Our path to get there involved hacking (i.e., a solution or workaround) the root causes of our problem.

I focused our leadership seminars on planning and running learning-centered meetings, building strong collegial relationships to help understand cultural differences, developing knowledge around leadership skills for each team leader, and modeling strong leadership skills during our seminars. Through an iterative process of testing ideas and gathering data, I was able to make decisions about which leadership hacks were worth sharing with others.

Leadership Hacks

One of the biggest challenges the teacher leaders faced was facilitation of meetings and decision making. The team leaders felt unsure about who needed to attend team meetings and how to make sure each team member had their voice heard. Our first hack was a simple yet powerful tool: conversation mapping. Over a week, I attended every grade-level team meeting. I drew a rectangle in my notebook to represent the table and each teacher's initials in the respective seating order around the table. Once the meeting started, I drew lines from the teacher's initials connecting who spoke, who responded, who spoke next, etc. I mapped the conversation for 20 minutes. When you look at the conversation map shown in Figure 15.1, you will notice that some people never spoke, some spoke twice, and some dominated the conversation. At our next

Cultivating Teacher Leadership

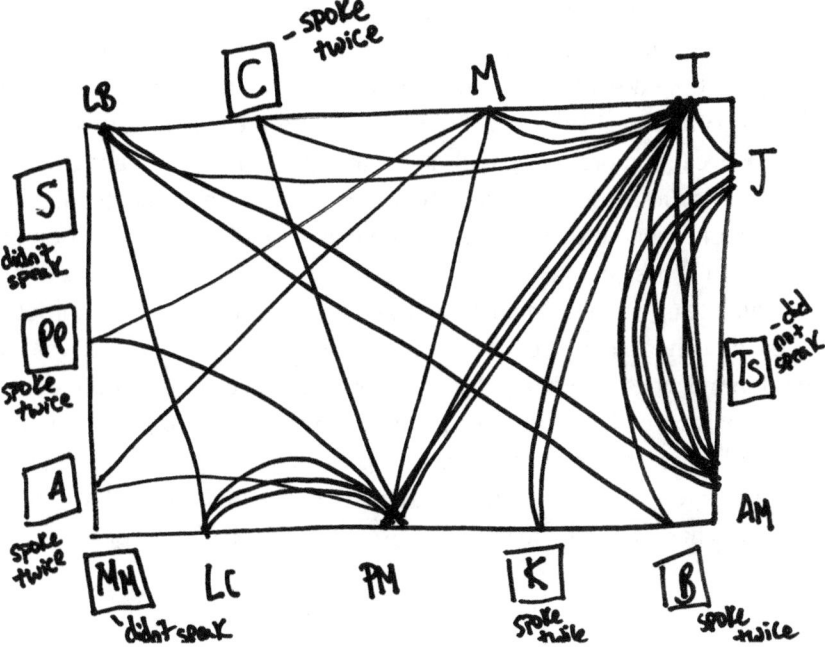

Figure 15.1 Conversation mapping

leadership seminar, we looked at the maps from each meeting. The data allowed the team leaders to reflect on their team meetings in meaningful ways. Each team leader used the agenda from the meeting to better understand why some people may not have spoken and why others seemed to dominate.

The data from the conversation-mapping hack informed the next leadership hack: meeting agendas. It was clear from looking at the different meeting agendas that key pieces of information were missing. For this hack, the team leaders were asked to add a purpose next to each agenda item (e.g., relationship building, learning, problem solving, decision making, information sharing, reflection/feedback, planning) and to include how much time they thought should be spent discussing each. This hack was transformational—such a simple idea that yielded powerful results. We were able to analyze how time was used in meetings as well as the topics being discussed. If the purpose of every item was information sharing then we discussed how to bring other topics into the team meeting such as learning from student work, eliciting team feedback on unit planning, etc. By adding a purpose to each agenda item, the team leader knew who needed to be present for the conversation and team members understood how to participate in the conversation in more meaningful ways. Team leaders became more thoughtful about the goal for each meeting, what items needed to be discussed to achieve the goal, and how much time the team should spend discussing items before either tabling the discussion or moving on to the next item.

Once team meetings had clear goals the team leaders set a purpose for each agenda item. We addressed the challenge of making all voices heard in meetings. The next set of hacks introduced a variety of protocols (e.g., decision-making protocols, student work protocols, and tuning protocols, etc.). The use of these protocols ensured that each person in the team had a role to play during discussions. Change to: Each hack we tried led to another hack. By the end of the semester, we had a set of powerful tools for cultivating teacher leadership.

What I Learned About Cultivating Teacher Leadership

At the end of the first semester, I saw a dramatic change in both the confidence of our team leaders as well as the quality of the grade-level team meetings. During our final meeting of the semester, team leaders reflected on the changes in their leadership practice. One team leader said that she created a shared agenda that has norms, topics, and the purpose of each topic. These changes allowed her to balance the types of topics and activities in meetings and her team knew what to expect before the meeting began. Another team leader said he started scheduling his meetings based on workflow ("Today we will look at stage 1 of our curriculum planning; next week we will look at assessments"). Thinking in advance about the tasks that support teaching and learning helped him to plan more meaningful meetings for his team. One final reflection shared by the entire team was the idea of asking for regular meeting feedback from their team through exit cards. The team leaders believed that the more information they could learn about their colleagues' experiences with the meeting process and meeting outcomes, the better they could lead their team.

Team Meetings Revisited

It was 1:15 pm, time for the grade-level team meeting to begin. I walked into the classroom, and almost all of the teachers were seated around the table sharing stories from morning recess. The team leader passed out copies of the meeting agenda as the last members of the team walked into the room and took their seats. The team leader thanked everyone for coming and read through the agenda. The team started with an activity called "connections" in which every member of the team had the opportunity, if they chose, to share something meaningful about student learning that occurred during the week. After five minutes, the team leader closed the activity and transitioned to the next item. Each item on the agenda was related to learning in some way. Teachers reflected on a unit that was ending that week and then made a plan for how they were going to launch their final unit of the year. The team followed the norms and the meeting ended on time. I smiled at the team leader and headed off to the next meeting.

Innovative Leadership Practices

If you are interested in putting these ideas into practice, the first step is taking the time to deeply understand your problem. The fishbone diagram protocol will assist you in determining a problem statement and identifying the specific categories that are contributing to your problem. Once you have mapped your problem, it is helpful to determine which of the specific categories contributing to your problems are causes and which are effects. The interrelational digraph protocol can be used to help you determine the root causes of your problem. Determining root cause(s) is an important step in the process because if you design hacks for the symptoms of the problem, your strategies are not likely to have lasting effects. A final protocol to help in your planning process is the theory of action protocol. This protocol will help you set a goal and identify a pathway for achieving that goal. The hacks I developed are specific to the problem addressed at my school. However, if you have similar problems, there are likely to be some hacks you can put into practice right away.

I implemented a variety of teacher leadership hacks over the course of a semester. I categorized them based on implementation effort and impact. For example, some hacks were very powerful and easy to implement while others were harder to implement but powerful.

I rated each hack as mild (low effort, low impact), medium (high effort, high impact), or spicy (low effort, high impact). Figure 15.2 is one example of a spicy hack.

This hack is SPICY

If you want teacher leaders to promote professional learning for continuous improvement try...

Conversation Mapping

What: Tool to understand who is participating in conversations during meetings.

How:

1. Jot down the initials of each person sitting around the table in the order in which they are sitting.
2. Decide how long you want to map the conversation.
3. Begin mapping! Each time someone speaks, draw a line from the person's initials who is speaking to the next person who speaks. Continue this process until your time is up or you believe you have a good sample.
4. Reflect: Did anyone dominate the conversation? Were there members who did not speak? How did participation impact the conversation? What might you do differently to either increase participation or balance participation?

Figure 15.2 Teacher leadership hack: Conversation mapping

> To access all of the hacks I developed visit www.kristenmacconnell.com. For free access to the protocols described above visit https://hthgse.edu/crei/protocols/. These protocols are copyrighted through Creative Commons.

References

Harris, A. (2014). Distributed leadership. *Teacher*. Retrieved from www.teachermagazine.com.au/articles/distributed-leadership

Von Frank, V. (2011). Teacher leader standards. *Learning Forward*, 6(5), 1–4.

Vignette: Distributed Leadership Through Reciprocal Advisory Structures

Joelle Basnight

> **Summary**
>
> This vignette explores how one principal built a system of advisory structures to increase student and teacher voice in shared decision making. These structures also served to build greater trust, empathy, and interdependence.

All too often, school policies and procedures are top-down. This approach can decrease buy-in and, at its worst, sour relationships between administrators, teachers, and students. In response, American International School Chennai's high school principal created two advisory structures that work together to include more voices in the school's decision making. In a high school of 210 students, of which around 20% of the multinational students change from year to year, such advisory structures represent an important and predictable way to invite student and teacher voice. By design, both structures implement the same innovation: distributing leadership to foster a stronger, more interdependent community.

The first advisory structure, the student advisory forum, comprises 22 students. Every August students apply to serve a 1-year term, with selection based on application quality and equal representation across grade levels. The principal, over time, delegates facilitation to two student mentors. In addition, mentors help younger members find their voice and gather input from and communicate decisions to the student body. Students who join the student advisory forum commit to group norms of collaboration and evaluate their use of them on a regular basis (see Figure 16.1). The agendas reflect authentic student concerns and have ranged from an overhaul of the tardy policy to food service quality. This structure nurtures trust and engagement while empowering a voice for decision making within the student body.

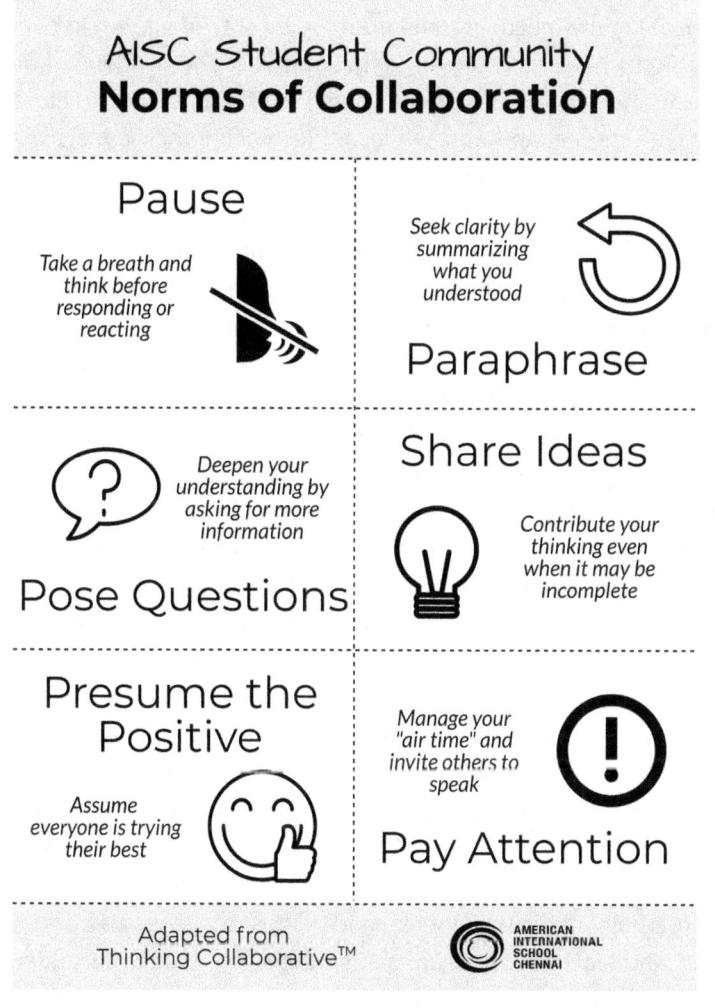

Figure 16.1 Norms of collaboration for the American International School Chennai (AISC)

The second advisory structure, the faculty community forum, processes procedural and policy matters, freeing faculty meetings to prioritize professional learning for teachers. Faculty members raise agenda items to be calendared and circulated for consideration. The faculty community forum convenes as needed, attracting only those interested in the agenda item, generally 10–40% of the faculty. Consistent communications remind faculty that all decisions made by the faculty community forum are final, and therefore teachers are expected to engage in the process or abide by the decision. Though it required an adjustment period, teachers grew to appreciate faculty meetings freed from topics only of interest to a few. Past agenda items have ranged from rethinking year-end academic honors to improving the process of student course registration. The structure treats faculty with respect and trust while still leveraging their collective intelligence to solve problems together.

Both structures support distributed leadership, transparency, and trust within the respective populations. Several times each year, however, an issue requires input from both students and teachers. Two years ago the faculty wrote a new assessment retake policy in support of mastery learning. Six months into implementation, it became clear that the policy was not working. The student advisory forum reported that teachers applied the policy unevenly, with some adhering carefully, others setting unofficial performance bars, and others refusing retakes altogether. After an initial dialogue, the student advisory forum suggested raising the issue to the faculty community forum and volunteers constructed a presentation of the students' concerns. Teachers attending the meeting listened and offered their own frustrations, including loopholes that they felt some students were exploiting. Realizing that both groups shared the same concern, they formed a small team of teachers and students to rework the policy.

The redrafting team began with further dialogue to better understand the issue. Students expressed concerns about the pressure to excel, and their sense that some used retakes as a means to avoid studying for the initial assessment. Faculty discussed feeling overwhelmed by retake requests and worries about creating authentic, fair retake options. The team then began revising, all the while seeking to address the stressors faced by both students and teachers. The team shared their final draft with students and faculty for comment. Not a single concern surfaced. The practice of collaborative, distributed leadership created the conditions that allowed quick resolution of a complex instructional challenge.

In sum, the advisory structures collectively allowed student and teacher voices to be heard while cultivating empathy and understanding across the groups. This not only improved the policy but also built community interdependence. Such a success fosters trust among students, faculty and administrators and lays a foundation for more effective, shared decision making in the future. Distributed leadership requires school leaders to cultivate an ethos of trust and collaboration and, most importantly, to believe that solutions are better found through dialogue than direction.

Innovative Leadership Practices

Linking innovation to practice is the result of applying new ideas and approaches in intentional ways that foster iteration and improvement. The leadership and innovation practices represented here are simple: *Trust your gut, do the research, and iterate with the help and support of others.* The hard work comes in the messy middle as you develop others to collaborate and find their own solutions. This takes tenacity, intentionality, and patience. The result is ultimately a more agile, resourceful community capable of coping with institutional change.

Creating a Culture of Learning

Ryan Elissa Hopkins-Wilcox

> **Summary**
>
> This chapter discusses how one international school created a culture of learning. The author explores how a change to the traditional model of professional development helped facilitate the growth of this culture. The author breaks the process into three interrelated parts: finding purpose, making connections, and building a culture of learning. She highlights areas for leadership within and provides examples of how her school made this possible.

As school leaders, we spend a lot of time discussing mission and vision. We know that a successful school is built on a clear sense of purpose and a plan to achieve that purpose. Most school leaders are also aware that creating a school culture is also crucial for school success. These ideas of purpose and culture are intertwined. The question before us as leaders is: What composes culture and how can we purposefully implement a cultural vision for our schools? The story that I would like to share in this chapter is one about finding purpose, making connections, and building a culture of learning.

The innovative practice I will be sharing in this chapter that has helped build a culture of learning in our school is what we call Personal Learning Journeys (PLJ). We wanted to build a culture where active learning is a continuous endeavor, not an occasional, passive experience. PLJ are a new model of professional development (PD) that allow for reflective,

Table 17.1 Moving from PD; Moving towards PLJ

Moving from PD	Moving Toward PLJ
Decreased emphasis on ...	**Increased emphasis on ...**
Compliance	Innovation, risk taking, commitment
A deficits model that identifies weaknesses to be "fixed"	Building confidence by identifying strengths to build on
Leader-directed learning	Agency (choice, voice, ownership)
Learning in isolation	Learning within a community
Teachers as passive recipients to learning	Teachers actively involved in reflecting on their own learning
Extrinsic motivation (rewards and appraisals)	Intrinsic motivation (autonomy, mastery, purpose)

Source: Pink, 2009.

teacher-directed inquiry. We wanted our teachers to embrace curiosity and to feel the joy of lifelong learning. To do this we looked at how our professional development was set up and we made changes. Instead of choosing learning based on weaknesses (what some call, in Professional Learning Communities, identifying problems in practice) we allowed teachers to choose their own learning journey as innovative practitioners building on their strengths as educators. Table 17.1 further outlines the shift in mindsets.

This chapter is the story of how our PLJ have helped us to find purpose, make connections and build a culture of learning. I will outline how we did this, in three sections: Finding Purpose, Making Connections, and Building a Culture of Learning.

Finding Purpose

The International School of Uganda (ISU) is located in Kampala, Uganda. It is a small, private school with 250 students, 45 staff members, and 25 teachers in the elementary section.

This innovative practice described in this chapter was a collaborative partnership between myself, working as the Assistant Principal/PYP Coordinator, and the elementary school principal, Daniel Todd.

When I joined the leadership team, Dan asked me what I'd like to do with the position. I knew that I really wanted to focus on inquiry-based learning and putting students at the center to honor motivation and lifelong learning. But in order to look at how inquiry and self-directed learning motivates students, I felt we needed to begin with teachers as self-directed learners. In essence, I wanted us to create a culture of learning for all learners. This was my purpose.

The saying "We teach as we were taught" is evident in many classrooms around the world as we look at the old "factory model of education" (Robinson, 2010) being replicated over and over again. And this continues while current research has been telling us for years that this model no longer works for our children and their future (see Bandura, 1997; Brandt, 1998; Csikszentmihalyi, 2004; Mitra, 2013, Papert, 1998; Richardson, 2018). I could hear the words of those who for years had inspired me in my own teaching: Malcolm Gladwell, Carol Dweck, Alfie Kohn, Taryn BondClegg, and Kath Murdoch among others. When I stopped to really listen, I understood that many teachers struggle to offer their students opportunities for self-directed inquiry when they work in environments that do not empower teachers to be self-directed learners. With perfect timing, the International Baccalaureate (IB) programme, through the Enhanced Primary Years Programme (PYP), brought forward the word "agency" for learning. The idea of agency is not new, but there is new life again for "agentic" learning. I knew, though, that we cannot expect student agency to be honored without teacher agency.

My goal was to offer teachers the opportunities to become agentic, self-directed learners connecting with their purpose and discovering the power of intrinsic motivation. Through PLJ we cultivate teacher agency by allowing choice, voice, and ownership in learning. I felt if teachers could themselves become inquirers, driven by their own interests, they could model and offer similar opportunities to their students. And together we could create a culture of learning where the learning is the work, the goal.

We spend time every year focusing on this idea of *purpose* in order to be able to allow for autonomy. I will walk you through a few protocols we have developed from our readings. But first let's discuss the importance of purpose. We believe that if we all understand our purpose and how we contribute to the shared purpose of our school, we then are able to confidently place trust in our teachers to choose their own inquiries for their PLJ.

We have supported teachers in finding their purpose by using a few different protocols. One method is to ask teachers to write their job description in one sentence (Bartlett, 2016). Another way to think of this is to consider what your own mission statement might be. Just as, in the business world, leaders work through these three prompts to find their mission and vison, we have used them to guide us in finding our purpose:

1. What do you do?
2. Who do you do it for?
3. So that …? (What do you hope is the result of your actions?)
   What + Who + So that = Purpose

A third protocol we followed for identifying purpose comes from the book *Switch: How to Change Things when Change is Hard* by Chip and Dan Heath. They suggest to first answer "What do you do?" Then keep asking "Why?" (e.g., Why do you do what you do? Why does it matter?). This is similar to the Five Whys protocol developed by Sakichi Toyoda, the founder of Toyota Industries, in the 1930s, an iterative, interrogative technique used to get to the core or heart of a topic. Finally, we have also used the words of Mark Twain as a provocation to inspire teachers to think about their true purpose:

> The two most important days in your life are the day you were born and the day you find out why.
>
> —Mark Twain

Thus, as PYP Coordinator and Assistant Principal, my role is to inspire and guide learning through passion, purpose, and inquiry.

To help teachers find out what is worth learning and meaningful to them we provided time for reflection coupled with materials to reflect on (e.g., school policy documents, learning principles, curriculum) and new research in education in the form of books, articles, and blogs to inspire new learning. To support strategies for learning we have had teachers plan their own unit of inquiry using the process of the PYP unit planner. This is guided by their interests (e.g., "What do you love to do?"), their passions (e.g., "What do you care about?"), their identities (e.g., "What makes you unique?") and their purpose ("How do the three questions connect to help you find out what you are meant to do?")

The most powerful of the protocols we used is based on Simon Sinek's book and TED Talk on the power of "why" (Sinek, 2009a; 2009b), We look

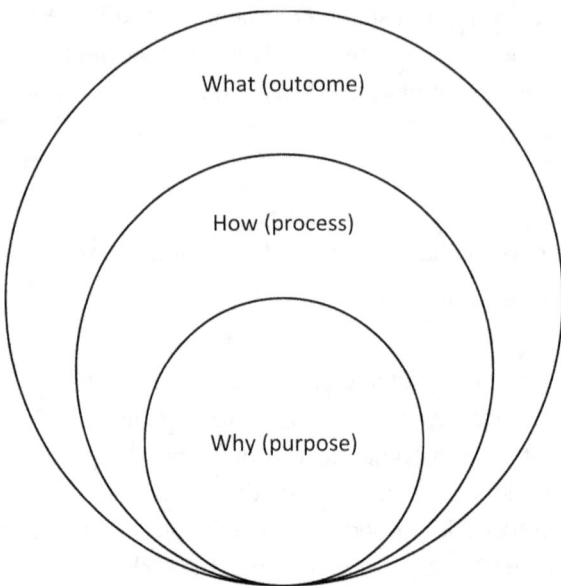

Figure 17.1 The Why, How, What components of learning

at the three components he suggests: why, how, what (see Figure 17.1). Starting with the why, we asked: "Why should teachers be learners?" We extended this to how: "How can teachers learn?" and finished with what: "What could teachers learn about?" We collaboratively filled in the why, how, and what, providing a list of inspirations for teachers to use to find their own purpose, process, and goal for learning.

Making Connections

Social constructivist theory posits that learning takes place through connections. Below I will share how we helped teachers construct meaning by providing connections. We did this, first, by making connections through interactions; second, by making connections to knowledge; and third, by making connections through experiences. We applied the same understandings of how children learn best to our teachers.

To make connections through interactions, we spent time looking at how we work together as teams in school and through partnerships. My principal and I drew on several areas of expertise. We used the Bonner Curriculum: True Color Personality Styles (True Colors: Exploring Personal

& Leadership Style, n.d.) inventory for self-awareness and team building. We took part in workshops on coaching in order to become peer coaches. We looked to the work of Marilyn Friend and Anne Benninghof for co-teaching models and Amy Edmondson for work on teaming. We connected teachers with each other for collaborative learning. We also realized that our learning community extends beyond the walls of our school. So we began connecting our teachers to others through social media and school visits. All of these connections and partnerships have contributed to enhance each of the PLJ.

Dan and I also connected teachers to current research in education. Our role as school leaders is to also be a leader of learning and to stay connected to our own learning in order to support others in their learning. We brought in texts for book studies, provided new frameworks and models to integrate, shared links and sites for research, and suggested courses and resources for learning. We also pulled from our own staff to honor the expertise within our school and make connections between people as resources for each other. Our teachers lead choice workshops which are like the ideas behind an "edcamp" or "unconference," and open their classroom doors to share practices with each other in structured sharing sessions.

To make connections between experiences, we provided teachers with the time to engage with their own learning by giving them back professional learning sessions. Accordingly, every Wednesday we have early dismissal for professional learning. This time is an essential resource for supporting PLJ. In addition, we dedicate time for guided reflection and further connections. Finally, we supported teacher initiatives as they applied their learning within our context. Some of the teacher PLJ have resulted in the creation of after-school activities, community events, new school committees, teacher-written blogs, the revision of school policies, participation in our school's lecture series in town, and more-active involvement in the school community. To allow for all of this to take place, we redefined leadership as shared connections between roles.

Building a Culture of Learning

While PLJ allow for a heuristic approach to adult education, the true purpose of the PLJ is to build a culture of learning within our school. Culture is defined as the beliefs, language, actions, and artifacts of a group of people or community. And so, to build a culture of learning we first had to build a community. The PLJ inspired teachers to become learners and to work in a community of learners. Shaping this community begins with bringing people on board, continues as we build capacity within our community, and culminates in the ongoing cultivation of relationships.

The culture of our school is reflected in our beliefs and values. As a leadership team, we guided our teachers through collaborative sessions to develop a shared language that reflects our beliefs. Together we defined what learner agency means for us, identified the purpose of school, developed beliefs about learning, and crafted our image of the child. We created a continuum for learning based on skill development through the grades, and wrote a philosophy for inclusive learning. These beliefs are lived out in our PLJ.

Our actions and artifacts further reflect our culture of learning. This is where you can see how our beliefs are lived. We created our own unit planner, which we call a "design for learning," to honor our belief about learning. Our grade-level teams take part in action research as pedagogical documenters. They observe learning, meet weekly to reflect, and collaboratively plan for future learning based on shared understandings of how children construct understanding. As a school we rewrite many of our policies and authored "Why Sheets" (see Kohn, 2019) to explain to our community our beliefs about learning. And most importantly, we are all active learners through our PLJ. We celebrated our teachers as learners by hosting a yearly "gallery" of learning in an atmosphere similar to an art opening where teachers share conceptual understandings about the process of learning and the art of teaching.

A core belief that holds our entire culture of learning together is our belief in the individual. This belief that everyone is a learner, a valued participant, and full of potential lays a foundation for trust. With trust teachers feel safe to take risks, try innovations, and learn from mistakes within and beyond their PLJ. As they learn to trust each other they collaborate and build a sense of collective efficacy. Teachers are valued as learners within a community which culminates in their ability to empower their students as learners and bring all learning forward.

When you have a true culture of learning at a school, the focus on learning becomes so powerful that there is less need for the formal evaluation of teachers. My principal and I have slowly been phasing out the traditional teacher appraisal process which focused on goal setting and product achievement in favor of dialog around the process and purpose of learning. To honor the science of motivation, we moved from external accountability through observations and checklists to internal accountability by cultivating intrinsic motivation. My principal and I now coach teachers through their inquiries to promote collective responsibility for professional learning and therefore success for all students.

A culture of learning in action

While we are never finished with our journey into learning, we can share some of the outcomes we have seen so far that let us know we are on the right path. Below are three stories from our community that reflect our culture of learning.

In our conversations with our teachers about the PLJ, one teacher told us that he was contemplating a new career because he no longer felt teaching fulfilled his needs as a "multipotentialite." But with the PLJ, a benefit of shared leadership within a community of learners is that he reconnected with his passions and purpose, and feels fulfilled in his career and inspired to continue following his passions as a learner both within and outside of school.

Every week we host a parent forum where we invite our community members to school to share in the learning with us. One week we had a request to understand more about how passions drive learning. We invited several students to form a panel for discussion. One question asked of a fifth grader was "What will you do with your passion in middle school when the learning is more teacher-directed?" The student responded, "I will simply continue learning and following my passion. I don't need school to help me with that. I am a learner on my own."

Additionally, one of our Grade 5 teachers (a native English speaker) wanted to take a course on English as an Additional Language (EAL). He did this, and now he offers adult English classes to our community members. In the traditional model of PD, we would not have selected an EAL course for that particular teacher, but by following his own journey he was able to find meaning in what he did and contribute to our collective purpose and culture of learning.

Lifelong Learning

As we continue reflecting on our learning through the implementation of our PLJ, we have ideas about where we would like to go next. In the coming year we will focus on our learning principle, Learning Is Lifelong. We will open up our PLJ to allow our teachers to learn *anything*. We want teachers who are excited about learning and can help our students to be inspired by their own interests and passions and empowered with learning skills, and ultimately to become self-regulated, lifelong learners. In order to do this, we need our teachers to themselves become reflective, empathetic learners, to journey alongside their students and better understand how we all pursue learning.

But to truly have a culture of learning situated within a community of learners we need to also begin looking at our whole community. We will focus on bringing everyone on board: bus drivers, cleaners, gardeners, administrators, parents, etc. We will begin as we did for our teachers by finding purpose in our community and as learners. We will then support everyone in making connections. And we will solidify our culture of learning through shared beliefs and values about learning with a common language that reflects who we are through our actions.

A great result of the PLJ was the breaking down of classroom walls and the de-privatization of learning. We would like to look next at how our PLJ can connect to the wider learning community to break down the walls of our school and partner with learners around the world in other schools. Would you like to join us in this journey? Come with us as we consider the future of school and learning. Let us establish a culture of learning and community of learners in a global movement to reimagine school.

Innovative Leadership Practices

The innovation referred to in this chapter is about creating a culture of learning through the process of reimagining adult learning, from professional development to personal learning journeys. To realize this, leaders should guide their entire learning community to find purpose, make connections, and develop a culture of learning. To find purpose, we recommend defining the purpose of school as a learning community and support individuals to find their purpose within the community and as a learner. These understandings can allow for autonomy and choice through trust, trust that we are all on the same journey.

A culture of learning and the successful implementation of PLJ is then dependent upon connections. School leaders have the crucial role of supporting and cultivating connections by fostering relationships and leveraging the power of networks through shared leadership within their community of learners. A culture of learning is further cultivated through shared beliefs, demonstrated by a common language, and lived through the actions of the learning community.

References

Bandura, A. (1997). *Self-efficacy: The exercise of control*. New York, NY: Worth.

Bartlett, K. (2016, September). *Writing a mission and vison*. Workshop presented at ISU in Kampala, Uganda.

Brandt, R. S. (1998). *Powerful learning*. Alexandria, VA: Association for Supervision & Curriculum Development.

Csikszentmihalyi, M. (2004, February). *Flow, the secret to happiness*. Retrieved from https://www.ted.com/talks/mihaly_csikszentmihalyi_on_flow?language=en

Heath, C., & Heath, D. (2011). *Switch: How to change things when change is hard*. Waterville, ME: Thorndike Press.

Kohn, A. (2019, March 6). *The Why axis*. Retrieved from https://www.alfiekohn.org/blogs/why/

Mitra, S. (2013, February). *Build a school in the cloud*. Retrieved from https://www.ted.com/talks/sugata_mitra_build_a_school_in_the_cloud?language=en

Papert, S. (1998, June 2). *Child power: Keys to the new learning of the digital century*. Speech presented at The Colin Cherry Memorial Lecture on Communication in U.K., London.

Pink, D. (2009). *Drive: The surprising truth about what motivates us*. New York, NY: Riverhead.

Richardson, W. (2018, October 4). *Learning today, learning tomorrow: Reimagining schools in the connected world*. Address presented at IB Global Conference: Shaping our Future in Austria, Vienna.

Robinson, K. (2010, October). *Changing education paradigms*. Retrieved from https://www.ted.com/talks/ken_robinson_changing_education_paradigms

Sinek, S. (2009a, September). *How great leaders inspire action*. Retrieved from www.ted.com/talks/simon_sinek_how_great_leaders_inspire_action

Sinek, S. (2009b). *Start with why: How great leaders inspire everyone to take action*. New York, NY: The Penguin Group.

True Colors: Exploring Personal & Leadership Style (n.d). Retrieved from http://bonnernetwork.pbworks.com/w/file/fetch/70546645/BonCur.TrueColors.pdf

18. Visiting Scholars: Bring Innovation to You!

Kimberly Ann Cofino

> **Summary**
>
> The Visiting Scholar program at Yokohama International School (YIS) brought leading educational voices into the small-school community from 2010 – 2013. As Visiting Scholars, these experts provided professional development for teachers and school leaders as well as highlighting the school in their studies. This vignette will describe the Visiting Scholar program and discuss its impact on the school.

From 2010 to 2013, Yokohama International School (YIS) in Japan implemented a Visiting Scholars program. This program invited educational researchers, in particular those looking to conduct studies in an international school environment, to work within the YIS community for short-term projects. As a smaller, somewhat geographically isolated, and highly innovative international school, YIS is well known for implementing this sort of small-scale, forward-thinking initiative. The Visiting Scholar program was designed to bring leading educational voices into the school community and to provide professional development for teachers and school leaders—all while encouraging these leading researchers to highlight the school in their studies.

Over the course of the three-year-program, YIS hosted a total of four scholars studying a wide range of topics, including: international schools, literacy, intercultural learning, and the International Baccalaureate Middle Years Program. Both the school and each scholar clearly benefited through these interactions. For the visiting scholar, YIS provided accommodation, round-trip airfare, and a modest stipend to cover living costs. In exchange, visiting scholars were expected to publish their results in an international education magazine or academic journal, to engage YIS staff in the area of research, and to provide some professional development sessions in their area of expertise.

The first visiting scholar to the program was Dr. Mary Hayden, a well-known author, researcher, and expert on international schools. While at YIS, Dr. Hayden met with teams of teachers from all divisions of the school. She ran parent and teacher professional development, observed in classrooms, and met with students and parents. During her time at YIS, she was provided with an office area on campus as a "home base" for her research. Her contributions included, for example, helping the school plan its Connected Learning Community 1:1 laptop program in a way that involved conscientiously seeking the opinions of every stakeholder group involved before the program began.

As a result of Dr. Hayden's visit, we implemented stakeholder case study groups to regularly record observations about changes in learning experiences for students, and these inclusive groups had a large impact on both the direction of the school's laptop program as well as the development of our iPad pilot program which began several years later. Without her insight, the school might not have been able to structure this kind of input and feedback so successfully.

YIS also hosted three other visiting scholars during the course of the program. Dan Shiffman focused on literacy and specifically the use of writing centers. Darlene Fisher investigated intercultural learning as part of her doctoral study through Bath University. Oli Tooher-Hancock visited with a focus on exploring the impact of the Middle Years Program in the International Baccalaureate. Through their work with the school, each of these scholars had a long-term impact—from influencing specific teaching strategies, to building community structures that value the diverse nature of the school, to deepening teacher understanding of the IB curriculum.

Unfortunately, YIS was not able to continue the program after 2013 due to changes in leadership and priorities within the school. Once James MacDonald, school head and the program's main advocate, left the school, other initiatives took its place under new leadership. However, feedback from both visiting scholars and stakeholders at YIS during and after this unique program's run was overwhelmingly positive, with consensus that the experience was valuable for all parties.

Innovative Leadership Practices

The Visiting Scholars program at YIS provided an interesting and unique model for professional growth and reflection. In order for this process to be successful, the school had to be willing to be closely observed by outsiders. More traditional school leaders might feel challenged by the inherent vulnerability of having academic researchers interacting with teachers, students, and parents, and this all took a form quite different from traditional professional development, which is often presented from a step-by-step practical perspective. However, not only teachers, but various groups of school stakeholders also found themselves involved in these reflective discussions. In the end, the Visiting Scholars program inspired new ways of thinking and elevated conversations throughout the school community.

Schools that prioritize innovation and the connection between the academic world and real-world classrooms should consider starting their own Visiting Scholar program or something similar. It is true that YIS is a private international school in a highly economically developed country, so this idea might initially seem impractical or cost-prohibitive for less well funded or non-international schools. However, the logistical setup of the program would not necessarily be much different from hosting a consulting visit, and might be combined with research or grant funding obtained by the school.

19 | A Reimagined Doctoral Program in Action: Confronting Equity Challenges in International Schools

Matthew Militello, Lynda Tredway, Tosca Killoran, Christie Powell and Kristin Halligan

Summary

Three doctoral students from the East Carolina University International Ed.D. program are featured in this chapter. They collaboratively engaged students, teachers, and/or parents in discussing and addressing practice-based issues. As a result, the three school leaders demonstrate the possibilities that emerged in increasing access and equitable participation for all school constituents. The findings suggest that teams of teachers, or parents, can collectively address equity challenges. This chapter provides vivid accounts of how participatory action research (featured as part of the Ed.D. design explicated in a previous chapter of this book) is applicable to school settings as a process for engaging all school constituents in school improvement through use of cycles of inquiry and analysis of qualitative evidence.

The purpose of this chapter is to provide accounts of what participatory action research with teams of Co-Practitioner Researchers (CPR) looks like in practice. Specifically, how do doctoral students engage in equity challenges as part of their research? More importantly, how is their work sustained in practice as international school leaders? Three vignettes, authored by students who have completed their Ed.D. at East Carolina University (ECU), set the stage for an analysis using the ECU reimagined Ed.D. as a framework.

Student Vignettes

Tosca: Finding Lǎoshī voice

My participatory action research project, set in two international school settings, had a clear focus on system and actions that perpetuate inequity. I began with teaching assistants in Thailand and continued in China. In both contexts, teaching assistants were initially hesitant to participate. Their reluctance was in stark contrast to the democratic inclusion espoused by their schools. I tapped into my knowledge of coaching, technology, and design-based pedagogies to facilitate a project that aimed to engage these teaching assistants.

The CPR team began with developing an understanding of self and others, through community learning exchanges (CLE). The CLE created a collaborative culture among local teachers, foreign teachers, leadership, coaches, and specialists. Relationships took center stage, and our objectives emerged naturally from deep listening. While the organizational and individual notion of equity was strong, initial data suggested voices were still silenced. The system continued to replicate inequities, and people were still fragile when confronted with their biases and behaviors. The fragility was particularly evident when the Chinese teaching assistants asked for their title to be changed from teaching assistant to Lǎoshī or "Teacher" in Chinese. They felt that it would be more honorific than the title of an assistant, which is complicated in the hierarchy of Chinese culture. One CPR member said, "I think it is important. First, it shows respect by using the host country language to address local staff. Second, it gives the school community an idea that teaching assistants should be respected as teachers" (personal communication, September 4, 2018). Another CPR member stated, "The greatest outcome of the CLE is that it has motivated people to speak up about their feelings ... not all positive, and from people who have previously remained quiet. For instance, the title change conversation has allowed for dissent and honesty, and we are learning more about the shades of equity in our community from people's reactions" (personal communication, September 3, 2018).

Our work yielded powerful reminders that leadership for systemic change needs incremental and co-designed protocols to be successful. In order to counter fear and uncertainty with joy and hope, we worked to frame our research in the assets and dreams of the local community. This enabled us to celebrate each shift that we observed. Teacher Erin Madonna stated:

> Greater awareness is absolutely blossoming within our community. Leadership has reached out to have conversations with us about future decisions and plans. The head of school has inquired about our work and has actively listened to the points of action we have raised. There are equity-focused professional learning opportunities facilitated by teaching assistants, teachers and members of senior leadership within the organization. Teachers are using the language of equity more frequently. People are sharing more openly about challenges they face in the workplace. Awareness is growing. Now, we need to move from awareness, to acceptance and action (personal communication, September 3, 2018).

The study countered silence by leveraging the local teachers' cultures, dreams, hopes, skills, and pedagogies as a voice for innovation within international schools. Through dialog, diverse networked communities were able to share insights and design, test, and create opportunities for change. The strategies shifted our community from a "them" to an "us" mentality, and from "for" to "with" advocacy.

Christie: Giving Alice a seat at the table

How can we build the capacity of international school teachers to improve the affective and cognitive learning of our increasingly diverse learners—culturally and linguistically? This was the focus of practice for two school years in a large (2900 students) international school where the language-learner population grew exponentially.

I worked directly with five teachers who taught sheltered English as an Additional Language (EAL) students. Using a "Map the Class" activity, I asked teachers to reflect on the cultural, personal, assets, and attributes of each student and to create a visual representation of the students. While the co-teachers were working to build caring communities of learners with the students, the evidence suggested that they were not fully drawing on the cultural and personal funds of knowledge that the students brought with them. As a result, they did not enact culturally and linguistically responsive practice in the classroom. In other words, students were the objects of instruction, not the subjects (Freire, 2000; Moll, Amanti, Neff, & Gonzalez, 1992).

In follow-up reflections after the mapping activity, a series of "a-ha" moments captured the overall realization about the lack of shared understanding about learners. The teachers realized that learners' profiles (e.g., assessment scores, cultural funds of knowledge, personal interests) did not seem to drive planning for learning. As a teacher stated, "The activity today raised a lot of 'wonderings' in me. As I create a profile for each of my kids in the class, I wondered if I am really representing the 'real' them. … I need to get to know them more. I want to represent them accurately and truthfully" (personal communication, January 27, 2018).

This was the starting point for the realization that students had a much bigger role to play in planning for learning. With the interests of students in mind, a Grade 8 language and literature unit took shape around the genre of fantasy instead of the dystopian literature that was originally planned. Earlier in the year, Alice had been a student of concern. In fact, in one planning meeting, a teacher indicated: "It's too hard for Alice to give us even a complete sentence." Yet, when she was engaged through a personal and cultural interest, she was able to clearly articulate her ideas.

In a planning meeting, the teacher commented, "Something Alice just sent me, made me cry. She shocked me … wrote a whole fantasy story. We would have never asked for an assignment like that" (personal communication, March 27, 2018). Alice wrote to her teacher, "I know my work is not good, but I kept writing and writing from my heart." Later that school year, Alice volunteered to read an entire essay in front of the class. Engaging students in culturally and linguistically responsive practice requires giving them a seat at the table and encouraging their voices. A teacher summed it up best: "I didn't realize how important it was to get that interest inventory from the students and how useful it is in grouping them and planning with that in mind … integrate and embrace the students' cultures into the lesson" (personal communication, May 20, 2018).

As the teachers and I examined planning practices, we noticed a significant change in the scripts of their planning meetings. In the first transcribed planning session, teacher talk was episodic and unfocused. However, over time we could see how teachers began to incorporate knowledge about students in their planning. Most significant in these data was the increase in the attention to scaffolding for student learning, higher expectations increased, and organizational task talk in the planning meeting decreased. Teachers came to understand the importance of knowing students' background, documenting it, and using it to plan for their education. The teachers noted that understanding and honoring the cultural backgrounds of the students helped them tap into student assets; instead of seeing language learning as a need, they began to see the richness of dual-language and multicultural experiences in classrooms. The process "made us understand that by not responding to students, it is we who are putting more barriers in front of them that hinder their learning" (personal communication, April 13, 2018).

Kristin: Connecting parents to our curriculum

This participatory action research project focused on how local school educators can co-create, and effectively implement, a transdisciplinary curriculum that aligned with and supported the International Baccalaureate Primary Years Programme (IB PYP) learner profile attributes, skills, and concepts. Inquiry-based learning emphasizes teaching students how to find out more, sort through information, and use that information to take action. Our team believed that a successful implementation of the curriculum would lead to improved teaching in order to improve student learning. Thus, our goal was that classroom learning be authentic, relevant, challenging, and meaningful.

The project began with the Grade 3 team of teachers and students at an international school in Bangkok. While the cycles of inquiry focused on teacher practices and student learning, one key component of the project was ensuring that the parents could articulate the rationale for a constructivist approach to learning and that they were fully engaged in the school as co-generators of building the kind of school environment in which all students experienced success. At our first parent workshop, teachers facilitated a mini inquiry to support parent understanding of "Who We Are" as a community. Together we engaged in a process known as KWL that engaged the parents in a community conversation about what they (K)new, (W)hat questions they had, and what they wanted to (L)earn. The parent workshop, designed to deepen our understanding of the inquiry-based transdisciplinary approach, paid off. The lines of inquiry that our parents developed were: (1) How do we transition to an IB school? (2) What is the difference between an education in our school and a more traditional education approach? (3) How do we best support our children at home in their learning journey?

In our second workshop, parents created posters highlighting their understanding of the differences between constructivist education and traditional education. Common themes indicated that they viewed educational as student-centered, interactive, and a creative education that focuses on how children use play to learn. By contrast, themes of traditional education indicated a teacher-centered approach that relied on examinations and grades. Because the parent workshop took on an inquiry approach, our parents came to understand our context and our work more fully.

The engagement seemed to empower parents to take further action. As one example, parents organized themselves and utilized the cycle of inquiry to address concerns about the food quality at our school. The parents observed the food each time they came to school for a special event or a parent/teacher organization meeting. One parent collected data, including photographs and observations. The parents group came to the conclusion that our school food was not up to the quality that they expected for their children. The parents researched catering companies and presented options to the school chairperson. Because of this cycle of inquiry, the school changed the caterer, and so enhanced the quality of school food. This is a powerful example of how parents can work together and act.

Analysis of Vignettes

The vignettes are rooted in issues of equity and utilized participatory action research (PAR) in which the researchers' work with Co-Practitioner Researchers (CPR) is highlighted. Doctoral students in positions of school leadership demonstrated a high degree of distributed leadership tenets by teaming with their colleagues as co-practitioner researchers at the beginning (deciding on a focus of practice together), middle (collecting and analyzing data), and end (co-generating implications) of their projects (see Spillane, 2006). The PAR projects focused on shifting the roles of teacher aides to co-teachers, using knowledge that teachers gained from mapping a class of English languagelearning students to plan and teach differently, and ensuring that parents were an integral part of understanding and contributing to a newly implemented program. In each story, there is an element of liberating voices. As a result, the voices of often-overlooked constituents in international schools became integral participants in the research process and changed practice and policy in their school communities.

Tosca's project gave voice to a marginalized group in international schools: teacher aides who are typically residents of the international school country. Tosca's study began at a school in Thailand and shifted to China when she changed jobs. While the context changed, the issues of marginalization did not. Tosca soon discovered similar issues across sites. With this knowledge, she and her co-practitioner researchers facilitated discussions and provided a safe place for teacher aides to engage in dialog. While the school structure did not change, the project raised awareness of the Lǎoshī voice in the school community. That awareness gave rise to changes in some teachers' practices with persons who were called aides and now viewed as co-teachers.

Christie's project with teachers resulted in realizations on the part of the teachers about how instrumental they could be collectively (Grubb & Tredway, 2010). The teachers' experiences with mapping and decoding their planning sessions matched their values about paying attention to students and resulted in changes in planning and classroom practices. However, the exponential number of English language learning (ELL) students now accepted at the school led to a substantial increase in ELL teachers (from five to twenty). As a result, the need to engage new teachers in the same experience overwhelmed the resources of the school, including the teachers and Christie. Yet, they were able to institute policies in the school that offer building blocks as the school finds its way to being more culturally and linguistically responsive.

Because Kristin's project was grounded in the IB philosophy that fits with the direction of the entire school, she and the teacher teams are continuing to demonstrate success in the designing and implementing the academic and social-emotional program for K–5 students. Because of the parent satisfaction at the school, enrollment numbers exceeded projections—even though parent voice has not been a part of the original plan. That result increases her action space for continuing to engage parents in cycles of inquiry as they become an intrinsic part of their children's PYP experience.

The findings from these studies are insightful and, at times, alarming. The main finding from the studies was: *We all need to listen to and learn with students, parents, and teacher aides in international schools.* PAR opened new opportunities and possibilities for dissertations embedded in one's specific place (context) and practice (content). Perhaps more importantly, the PAR projects demonstrate promise for a new level of collaboration with co-practitioners' research partners as well as other PAR participants, including parents, other teachers, and students. This is quite different from the hierarchical structure of most international schools, and the processes show possibility of moving the tenets of distributed leadership to the international school arena.

Innovative Leadership Practices

What we learn—knowledge—is important, but *how* we learn is probably even more so, because it has the power to increase knowledge and enlarge perspectives. If our belief system relies on a philosophy of dialog that forwards a "non-banking" form of education and if our principle about how change happens with and through individuals and groups (relationships) is right, then the programmatic structures have to match and model our belief system (Freire, 2000). We found the projects are striking at the triple aims of our ECU Ed.D.: (1) emancipating marginalized local voices, (2) focusing on improvement efforts rooted in an issue of equity, and (3) changing the practice of international educators through a deep reflection of practice that provides tools and processes necessary for school leaders to understand, honor, engage, and collaborate with new places and people as is the case with international educators.

In the end, each vignette provides a vivid account of what innovative leadership for learning looks like in practice. Educational leaders are relentlessly challenged to bring a vision to life, make marked improvements in student learning, build relationships with the entire school community, and remain centered on equitable practices and outcomes. Our data suggest that the road to such innovative leadership for learning practices is paved by:

- Understanding that knowledge is co-generated (Bransford, Brown, & Cocking, 2000; Freire, 2000; Vella, 2008);
- Learning about self as a necessary act in supporting organizational change (Guajardo, Guajardo, Janson, & Militello, 2016);
- Honoring local wisdom and the context of the place in which we work (Guajardo et al., 2016);
- Engaging with a steady, yet balanced diet of inquiry and action—asking and doing (Dewey, 1938; Freire, 2000); and
- Leading with considerations of equity, cultural knowledge, and responsiveness with a social justice frame of reference (Gay, 2000; Gooden & Dantley, 2012; Theoharis, 2009).

The structure of the program has set the necessary conditions for innovative leadership for learning. However, learning from the scholar-practitioners highlighted in this chapter who did the work supports the importance of "on the ground" learning in which all Ed.D. programs can and should engage. The research processes are thorough, thoughtful, and informative. And, perhaps most importantly, because of the support and the tenor of the Ed.D. program, they collectively supported each other to have the courage to confront equity challenges in their contexts.

References

Bransford, J., Brown, A., & Cocking, R. (2000). *How people learn: Brain, mind, experience, and school*. Washington, DC: National Academy Press.

Dewey, J. (1938). *Experience & education*. New York, NY: Touchstone.

Freire, P. (2000). *Pedagogy of the oppressed* (30th Anniversary ed.). New York, NY: Continuum.

Gay, G. (2000). *Culturally responsive teaching: Theory, research, and practice*. New York, NY: Teachers College.

Gooden, M., & Dantley, M. (2012). Centering race in a framework for leadership preparation. *Journal of Research in Leadership Education, 7*(2), 237–253.

Grubb, W. N. & Tredway, L. (2010). *Leading from the inside out: Expanding role for teachers in equitable schools.* New York, NY: Paradigm Publishers.

Guajardo, M., Guajardo, F., Janson, C., & Militello, M. (2016). *Reframing community partnerships in education: Uniting the power of place and wisdom of people.* New York, NY: Routledge.

Moll, L., Amanti, C., Neff, D. & Gonzalez, N. (1992, Spring). Funds of knowledge for teaching: Using a qualitative approach to connect homes and classrooms. *Theory into Practice, 31*(2), 131–141.

Spillane, J. (2006). *Distributed leadership.* San Francisco, CA: Jossey-Bass.

Theoharis, G. (2009). *The school leaders our children deserve: Seven keys to equity, social justice and school reform.* New York, NY: Teachers College Press.

Vella, J. (2008). *On teaching and learning: Putting the principles and practices of dialogue education into action.* San Francisco, CA: Jossey-Bass.

SECTION VI

Technology and School Leadership

Introduction to Section VI: Technology in Schools

In a few of my past articles, I have stressed that technology leadership is just good leadership. This being so, the good leaders highlighted in this section also espouse that belief. Whether it is through rethinking space and place or if it is through reimagining initial teacher support, innovative school leaders understand that technology can be beneficial.

In this final section, the focus is on the nexus of technology and school leadership. In Chapter 20, Shwetangna Chakrabarty discusses how her school used design thinking to rethink technology of learning spaces. She explores how school leaders can lead in the transformation of the learning spaces to promote inquiry and enhance student engagement. In Chapter 21, Todd Von Seggern focuses on how leaders should think of digital technology as an omnipresent tool rather than one relegated to certain rooms. He discusses how technology has been used in his school to empower teachers, students, and administrators. Jeff Dungan, in Chapter 22, writes about an online teacher induction program developed at the Shanghai American School in China. He explores how this course came to be, how it was rolled out, and what improvements are on the horizon. Jeff lays out the content of each model and discusses what worked and what did not.

Modern technology affords opportunities for a wide array of innovative practices. This was evident in these international schools. In the chapters in this section, the authors noted how leaders can use principles of design thinking to rethink and link the analog and digital worlds. Technology can be used as a tool of empowerment for teachers, students, and leaders. As with many innovations, a common theme in these chapters was that leaders need to accept the fact that risk and failure are norms. Innovative leaders have to embrace both! And ... they have to do it while fostering distributed leadership throughout the organization.

Innovative Learning Spaces: Design Thinking in Pedagogy

Shwetangna Chakrabarty

> **Summary**
>
> At present, international schools around the world have invested a lot in physical learning spaces as they can be considered the core space for teaching and learning. Questions arise: Why is this space so crucial to how we teach and learn? How can we integrate the learning space into our pedagogy? What are the benefits of exploring learning spaces? This chapter discusses why, how, and what design thinking can do to enhance pedagogy in any school environment. It will focus on how leadership decisions can transform the learning spaces in dynamic spaces to promote inquiry and enhance student engagement.

Our school, Dar es Salaam International Academy, is a mid-sized international school in Tanzania, Africa. It is diverse, with 40 different nationalities in a population of approximately 300 students. As an International Baccalaureate Diploma Program (IBDP) Coordinator, one of my leadership goals was to explore the potential of learning spaces in my school. The primary reason for devising a leadership strategy to focus on the learning spaces was limited resources due to the country contexts. The best way forward was to work with available space to rethink its usage. The process of redesigning learning spaces started off with a survey given to teachers in and outside our school. Looking at the survey results, it was clear that despite multiple contemporary spaces being available within the school setting, teachers were not experimenting with it. In discussion with the school pedagogical team, it was decided that teachers should be encouraged to showcase best practices by modifying the learning space. Hence, we started the journey of design thinking in pedagogy.

A simple example of design thinking in pedagogy is a campfire site as a learning space. This setup is a classic example of the earliest kind of innovative learning spaces. These types of spaces evolved into simple classrooms with basic facilities to deliver teaching material. Depending on the nature of the evolving space, the teaching pedagogy evolved too. In schools, physical spaces are being redesigned, deconstructed, and reconstructed in order to evolve into a new space to ensure learning happens meaningfully and effortlessly.

In the past two decades, the physical learning space has taken a huge leap and evolved in a dynamic, mobile, flexible, less structured, and more connected space with the help of technology—hence the term *digital learning spaces*. The digital and the physical learning spaces together create the innovative learning spaces in our school. The structure of conceptual learning explains that knowledge is acquired when the overlapping of skills, content, and concepts happen in a learning space. For us, the question was how to create a learning space that facilitates this process. I proposed a riff on the TPACK framework, which posits that learning with technology is an interplay among understanding technology, mastering content, and applying pedagogy. I modified and renamed it "SPACK," an acronym for *space, pedagogy, and conceptual knowledge*. Combining the forces of conceptual understanding of TPACK, I created my own strategy Venn diagram (Figure 20.1). This framework was adopted as a strategy by the leadership team to guide teachers in innovating with how they used learning spaces.

SPACK is an easy tool all teachers can use. They need to decide what concept/content/skill they want to teach, then plan the method (i.e., pedagogy) of delivering it. Teachers fill in the Space circle by identifying the most relevant and appropriate space to teach the concept/content/skill with the selected pedagogy. Here is an example. If you want to teach refraction and reflection (the content) by modeling (the pedagogy) the experiment you plan to use the physics lab (the space) to teach this concept. Thus, SPACK is a simple tool to help teachers to meaningfully associate and integrate

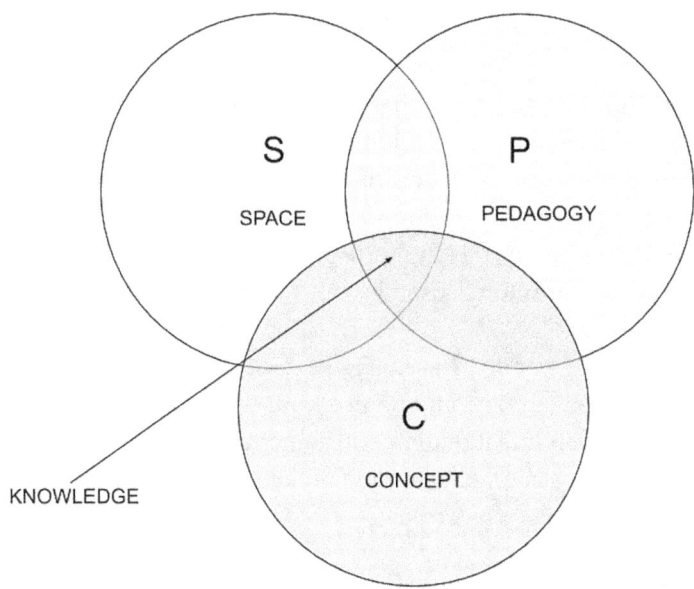

Figure 20.1 Space, pedagogy, and conceptual knowledge venn diagram

space with teaching and learning. The simplicity of this strategy made it easier to apply by drawing three circles, filling in the first idea, and letting the others just flow.

Let us now look at strategies that were discussed with the teaching team in order to develop a relationship between space and pedagogy under the lens of the International Baccalaureate (IB) framework with both approaches from physical and digital learning spaces.

Design Thinking in Physical Learning Spaces

The IB pedagogy allows flexibility of space, student choice, student agency, differentiation of instruction, integration of multiple disciplines, and a focus on individual or small-group rather than large-group instruction. This has led the school leadership to focus on enhancing the physical learning spaces that can accommodate the IB philosophy. Some examples practiced in our present classrooms as it relates to space and design thinking are below.

The emergence of a smarter classroom

The classroom is now a smart space that caters to diverse student needs. Here it is essential to emphasize on the ergonomically designed, flexible furniture that changes the shape of the classroom as planned by our teachers. The teacher can decide to create multiple formations to play with multiple pedagogies. Figures 20.2, 20.3, 20.4, and 20.5 illustrate dynamic classroom settings used by our teachers and the purpose they fulfill.

The first setting "sage on the stage" (Figure 20.2) is used for lecturing when teachers have limited time and do not want students to work independently without much collaboration with other students. Though this type of arrangement doesn't facilitate differentiation, it is suited for our

Figure 20.2 Sage on the stage

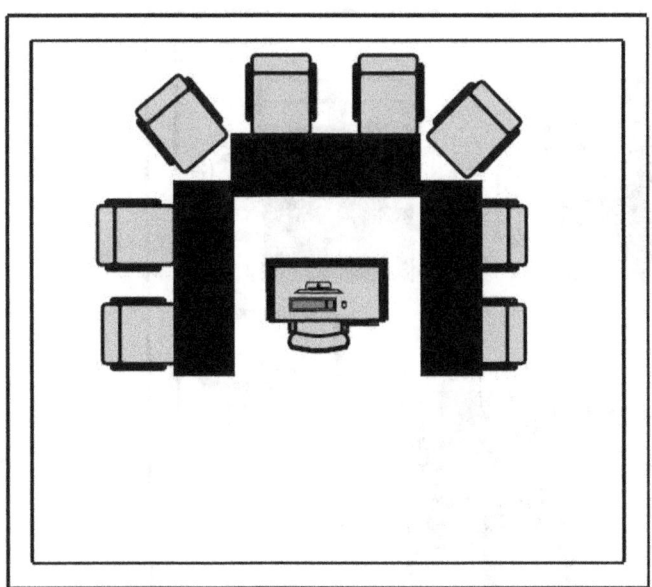

Figure 20.3 In the bowl

Figure 20.4 Roundtable conferencing

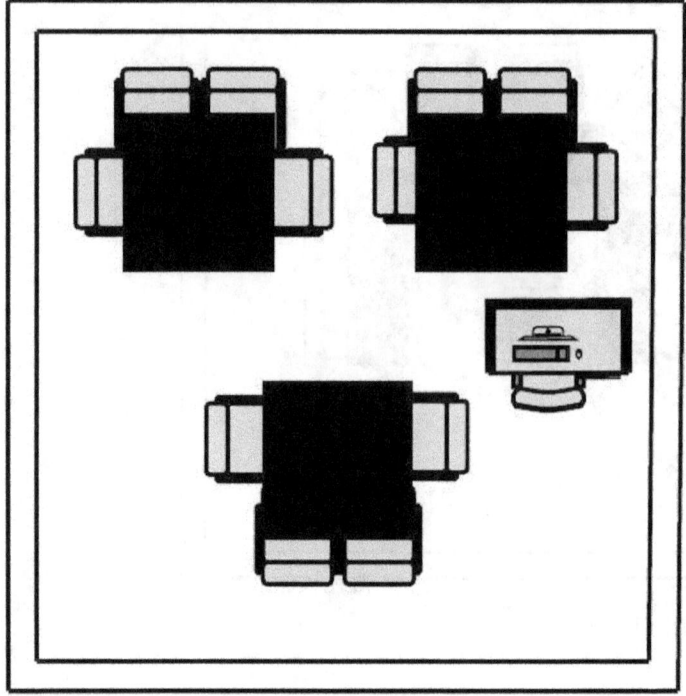

Figure 20.5 Guide on the side

senior students, allowing them to develop focus and content knowledge. The second setting "in the bowl" (Figure 20.3) allows the teacher to reach out to each and every student. It is our team's favorite arrangement for review, quizzes, and Q&A as it promotes critical thinking and allows our teachers to go deep into the bowl as well as to the top. The third setting "roundtables" (Figure 20.4) is a conference-style arrangement great for collaborative projects. It is predominantly used when teachers plan for group activities. This arrangement facilitates a carousel approach where groups of students move from one roundtable to the other. This arrangement is most suited for middle school students and helps in developing social and communication skills. And finally, the fourth setting "guide on the side" (Figure 20.5) is practiced for research activities or inquiry. Stations set up for students to complete a task in groups or pairs. Our teachers explicitly point out the seating arrangement for each unit and lesson they plan.

Classrooms as research hubs

The IB Programme utilizes a skills-based approach. One of the most essential skills nurtured through the IB Programme is the ability to do research with an increasing shift towards using information resources. Hence, the ability to research is the deciding factor in the learner's success. This being the case, the leadership decided to reconstruct the learning spaces in our school to facilitate the research process and allow for access to research material using technology and for seamless connectivity with the internet; and of course the teacher just acts as the guide to direct the research process. As a result, our classrooms are designed to act as research hubs where learning is led by students.

Interactive collaboration project focused approach

Research shows that students learn best in a collaborative environment. One of my leadership objectives was to shift from creating a collaborative environment to creating a culture of collaboration. In creating this culture, the role of space was pivotal. An open school without walls is an excellent example of learning through collaboration. Creating space for multidisciplinary or interdisciplinary collaborative projects is our new approach to learning. The easiest way to do this is to plan collaboratively to invest in a space that allows flexibility. For example, sliding walls between classrooms create flowing spaces allowing students access to arts and technology in a single space. Project spaces, or hubs, are a few great ideas to facilitate students to collaborate with each other regardless of the disparity in age, task, and ability. As an instructional team, we are planning interdisciplinary lessons that can be taught in a common space without walls.

Explicitly reinforcing skills

The Approaches to Learning within the IB curriculum are broadly categorized into five skills: thinking, researching, communicating, collaborating, and socializing. Physical learning spaces directly impact the facilitation of these skills. Our classroom spaces are now more dynamic to allow students to identify their learning preferences and learn accordingly. An example that we practice in our classrooms is to create different skill hubs. A research hub has power connections, a computer, and good Wi-Fi reception. A collaboration hub is closest to the whiteboard with lots of writing material and a roundtable with chairs around it. The social hub is a comfortable space with comfy cushions or sofas and a carpet to sit down and be able to listen to each other. These are some simple strategies that can be easily adopted by any school in any context.

Design Thinking in Digital Learning Spaces

With the integration of technology, our classrooms are being catalyzed into digital learning spaces. With the leadership strategy focused on integrating technology in learning spaces, here are a few examples that can be used by any school that has access to digital tools.

Flipped classrooms

The ability to teach without being present is one of the biggest advantages of digital learning spaces. Remote classrooms are facilitated by recording the lesson and sharing it with the students. This approach allows our teachers to delve deeper into the concept as the content has been received via shared videos; this way our students come to the lesson well prepared and ready to develop higher-order thinking through meaningful discussions. This *flipped classroom* approach is a very common and successful integration of technology into our classroom space across all disciplines. Videos are now part of our school's teacher toolkit. The school has a teacher toolkit on the website which is accessible via a login and password. It houses all flipped-classroom videos and other digital tools created by teachers to support and enhance the teaching and learning experience. The teacher toolkit can also be downloaded and stored offline in case there is no internet and teachers need to access those resources. This toolkit has been developed by teachers for teachers. The school leadership supports this initiative by encouraging teachers to share best practices and record their best lessons in order to upload to the teacher toolkit.

Visible thinking tools

With the influx of apps and extensions, technology-integrated classrooms allow the use of visible thinking tools like Padlet. We use Padlet in our classrooms to help students share and transfer knowledge via visible thinking. This is a great tool as it helps students to build memory and learn by triggering the interconnections in the brain. It is easily incorporated into the learning space.

Fostering inclusion

International schools are collaborating with each other on various projects to enhance the learning experiences of all students. Recently, our Diploma Programme students went to Berlin, Germany to work with a refugee aid focus group to learn how to plan sustainable community service projects. This opportunity was available through online collaboration with an online CAS (creativity, activity, and service) tour organizer. These are examples of inclusion and celebrating diversity by crossing borders both virtually and physically. Being internationally minded is deep-rooted in our school philosophy. We are using technology to create a pedagogy that is internationally relevant by engaging with a worldwide audience.

Circular learning model

As an international school teacher, "I have created my own mode (see Figure 20.6) inspired by the IB inquiry cycle and Simon Sinek's Golden Circle (Sinek; 2011). It reinforces that the power of questioning is the core of all teaching and learning. When learning spaces are designed with the purpose of facilitating learning, it caters to various learning needs. Our teaching team is on board with this philosophy as we regularly reflect on why we use a certain kind of space and how we can design learning spaces to make it more relevant to teaching a concept.

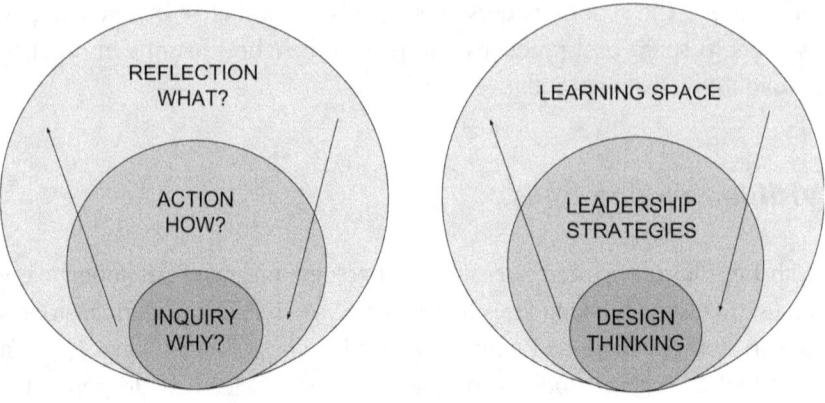

Figure 20.6 Circular learning model

Enhanced peer interaction and collaboration

Digital learning spaces enable simulations required for a real-life application of skills. It is the integration of the digital with the physical learning space that makes pedagogy creative. Our school has successfully implemented the no-wall classroom by introducing *Intrinsic Motivation Week*. Here, students are given the freedom and space to learn whatever they want to learn, from playing instruments to cooking to building robots. They can decide what they want to learn. Students move between classrooms to consult teachers, use the labs to research, use the canteen space to cook, use the rooftop gardens to do science experiments, or use the playground to learn basketball/football skills. At the end of the week, students showcase their learning or newly acquired skills.

Innovative Learning Spaces: A Design Thinking Pedagogy

The most innovative space is the cognitive learning space or the mind, I like to call this the *workspaces of the mind*. Research shows that you can become reasonably good at *any* new skill in 20 hours (Kaufman, 2014). Students should be given the opportunity to learn anything they want to learn. The workspaces of the mind use cognition to create metacognition. This technique works on memory retrieval (Ron, 2006). Here the mind is the learning space; teachers need to activate it through memory retrieval like creating visible thinking routines. Below are a few examples from my current school of how, as a curriculum leader, I have modeled my lessons to trigger the workspace of the mind.

Turning space into visible thinking tools

Students find it extremely challenging to master and understand concepts. I have done many experiments to ensure students understand concepts quickly. One of the best ways to do it is to make students create mind maps of the program requirements by reading the guides. In the first week, students read subject guides and create a curriculum map for the classroom display, making the walls into visible thinking tools. This helps students to visualize the subject content, concepts, and requirements. I also paint one wall black and allow students to use color chalk to explain their conceptual understanding or to simply do long mathematical calculations.

Integrating technology into art and art into technology

Space can be modified easily to suit the learners need. For one of my math topics, we were looking at string art. Students had to apply their knowledge of integration to generate area under graphs and then create interesting string art. To facilitate this process, I divided the math classroom into two parts by using big display boards as separators. On one side, students worked on displaying graphs and on the other side they set up a mini art lab with long desks, to work on the string art pieces. This created a space where technology led to art and art represented technology seamlessly. Space created an environment conducive to students' understanding how technology and art are complementary.

Using digital space to collaborate and communicate

For my business management Grade 12 class, I use Facebook as a teaching and learning platform. I created a closed Facebook group to include all my business management students. I post interesting articles, TED talks, and case studies supplemented by three questions on each post. Students must comment after analyzing the post. This is both engaging and relevant use of digital space; students prefer this platform and indulge in meaningful conversations. Here is a reflection from one of my business management students:

> We are asked different questions on the case studies or videos that Ms. Shweta uploads every week. We have to comment on it. I have learned so much just by reading my friends comments. I somehow remember everything better and now I don't feel like I am wasting time on Facebook. All these comments are like notes I can use for revision.

After this successful experiment, I want to partner with teachers/students from other schools to use social media learning space as a classroom.

The Community Is the Most Ancient Learning Space

Our students work very closely with the community. As they approach graduation, it becomes mandatory to record community service and engagement as a part of their core curriculum requirement for the IB Diploma Programme. Students have always benefited by utilizing the space in the school and outside the school to either bring in the community or take their learning out to the community. Reaching in and reaching out has been the most significant learning experience. Here are a few examples.

Reaching in

Our students created rooftop gardens with the help of a parent who has gardening expertise and knowledge about plants. This space has transformed into a green haven where members of the school community can go and relax or just enjoy the beauty of nature. Math and science topics have been taught with the rooftop garden as a project such as the topic of measurement in math and osmosis and germination in science. This project allows students to experiment, learn by doing, realize measurable goals, and get a sense of accomplishment by utilization of available space in the best possible way. For teachers, it is a great way to move outside the classroom to include the environment we live in into their pedagogy.

Reaching out

The Grade 11 students planned to contribute toward raising money for children who are born with hydrocephalus and spina bifida, which is a dire issue in Tanzania. Students began by raising awareness within the school and outside the school to collect cash and materials in order to help the children and their families. They set up donation boxes at various malls, shops, and stores in Dar es Salaam clearly explaining the cause. In this way, they also raised awareness within the wider community about the issues. Within the school, students led awareness programs during homerooms, assembly, lunch, and breaks. They came up with a *flexicard scheme* to ensure students participate in and contribute to this cause. If a student donated anything over $25, they would get a card that had benefits such as homework pass, free dress day, and free time from lessons. It was a huge success! The students were able to collect a substantial amount, and material such as soaps, sanitary pads, and a wheelchair. This happened because the school provided a space to bring this project to fruition.

> ## **Innovative Leadership Practices**
>
> The innovative practices highlighted in this chapter focus on leadership decisions of experimenting with the space. By adopting the simple models, schools can easily modify learning spaces to create innovative learning spaces. The models and approaches discussed in the chapter can be implemented in any context in any school if there is a will to experiment. The leadership strategies need to be mission-led and vision-driven, the mission being to enhance student engagement and learning and the vision being to redesign the learning spaces creatively. The quest to modify, create, design teaching space to enhance learning has led our school to create design thinking pedagogy. As our leadership mantra says: Be a risk taker and create your own learning space!

References

International Baccalaureate. (2015). *Approaches to learning*. Retrieved from https://xmltwo.ibo.org/publications/DP/Group0/d_0_dpatl_gui_1502_1/static/dpatl/guide-teaching-based-on-inquiry.html

Kaufman, J. (2014). *The first 20 hours: How to learn anything...fast*. New York, NY: Portfolio.

Kelly, M. (2019). *Bloom's taxonomy—Application category and examples*. Retrieved from https://www.thoughtco.com/blooms-taxonomy-application-category-8445

Open Learning (2019). *Value of digital learning for students*. Retrieved from https://openlearning.mit.edu/value-digital-learning-students

Sinek, S. (2011). *Start with why*. Retrieved from https://www.ted.com/talks/simon_sinek_how_great_leaders_inspire_action?language=en

Technology in Today's Schools
Todd Von Seggern

Summary

This chapter discusses the importance of incorporating technology into our schools and classrooms outside of the technology lab environment. Technology should be readily available to students so that we can prepare them for a successful future where they can self-regulate their use of technology and also learn the skills that allow them to use technology meaningfully and successfully. Key stakeholders need to be involved in order to foster a positive environment for our students. These stakeholders include teachers, administrators, and parents as well as the students themselves.

Just over ten years ago the world's first smartphone hit the market. The iPhone had a touch screen, the first of its kind, and was internet-connected at all times. Suddenly, we had unprecedented access to the entire internet in our hip pocket. This meant that every child under the age of ten would grow up in the age of smartphones and internet connectivity. The trends are not moving backward. Indeed, we are looking at a future of increased connectivity and automation in our lives. The question arises: What does that mean for education? How are we equipping our students for the digital age?

The International School of Uganda is an International Baccalaureate Continuum School with over 500 students where 250 students are in the elementary school. My role is that of the technology integrator and instructional coach in the elementary school. The school currently has 2:1 iPads in our classrooms from Early Years to Grade 3 and we have a 1:1 laptop program for our students in Grades 4 and 5.

At our school, the teachers, administrators, and I began by gathering observations, and we noticed the digital age all around campus. Our elementary students were bringing phones and tablets to school. After school, we began to see some of our youngest children interacting with their parents' smartphones as their parents met with teachers or were chatting with each other. In class, students shared stories of computer games and YouTube videos. When talking to our students, we found that most of them had access to some device at home, whether it was a phone, tablet, laptop, or video game console. What were they doing on these devices? Well, the answer was varied and complex, but it distilled down to the fact that most were not being very productive, and some were being unsafe. So what were we doing as a school to help our students be positive digital citizens? We took one look at our computer lab with its fingerprint-smeared monitors and confirmed that we were certainly not helping much.

Thus, we began a journey of transformation. As educators, we wanted to bring the 21st century to our school and prepare our students to be successful in the age of digital immersion. We wanted our students to be not just simple consumers of technology, but rather empowered creators who could use a variety of skills and technologies to communicate and create.

Along this journey, we realized pretty quickly that our students were only one part of a group of stakeholders at our school. It became apparent that all members of our school needed to be empowered in order to have a lasting impact. These stakeholders, in addition to our students, were the teachers, administrators, and parents. It is around these stakeholders that I would like to structure this chapter. I will discuss how students, teachers, administrators, and parents at the International School of Uganda forged amazing relationships and truly impacted how technology is used by our students, both at school and at home. I will share some of the key strategies and lessons that we learned along the way.

Empowering Students

When we imagined the world we live in, with technology surrounding us, we realized that we needed to create an environment for our students that mirrors the reality of today. We began by phasing out our IT lab so that we could introduce tablets and laptops into the classrooms. We wanted to bring the tools of the IT lab into each classroom so that they were available to the students at all times, not just once or twice a week. Unsurprisingly, we found that the students loved to use the devices and much positive energy was created in our learning environments. Surprisingly, because the devices were available at all times, the students were more willing to share and work together on them. Amazing collaborative opportunities arose, and the students became more passionate about learning because they could pursue a variety of inquiries. We also saw that students became excellent teachers of technology. They would share new tools and find better ways to complete tasks. Teachers fostered these opportunities by highlighting expertise in the classroom and encouraging students to use each other as resources. We have our 5th-graders teach our 3rd-graders to use apps on the tablets. We have our middle school students help lead our robotics clubs and coding classes.

The prevalence of devices in the classroom also gave us opportunities to build digital citizenship into our daily routines. The students and teachers worked together to create "Essential Agreements" for their classes. Each Essential Agreement is a set of behaviors and rules that are created by the students and their teachers in every class. One might think of it as a collaborative set of class rules. The Essential Agreement is signed by all members of the class and posted on the wall throughout the year for reference. Out of these agreements come excellent discussions where students learn about the dangers of too much screen time, the importance of exercise, internet safety, having positive interactions online, and much more. Importantly, these discussions establish an open atmosphere where we can speak freely about technology without worry.

Every journey is not without its challenges, and there have been some great learning moments for us, with more coming all the time. One discovery was that our students carried a prevailing attitude that tablets and laptops were entertainment tools. Because of this, we built lessons to show the students how to create products rather than consuming websites and videos. As a result, the students are now making movies, books, slideshows, 3D designs, and video games to show their learning.

We also learned that the internet is a hard place to do research. The internet, as we all have experienced, is a place where one can easily follow a path to nowhere! Because of this, we curated lists of appropriate websites for each unit that our students can visit and learn about the topics they are studying. Access to these sites is available on every tablet and laptop, so it does not matter what device they happen to pick up.

Lastly, we learned that we needed to redefine what we understood "technology" to be. On our journey to help the students use technology to create products, we found that not all products could be made on a device. Sometimes kids wanted to manufacture or build something to test an understanding or show learning. Out of this, we developed a Makerspace that provides our students with a place to come tinker, build, and create designs for their units of inquiry. We repurposed our old IT lab as the Makerspace, which feels quite poetic.

We are now in our fourth year of this journey, and our classrooms have completely transformed. Throughout the day, I am in and out of many classes. I get to see the magic our teachers are fostering. Students are using books, paper, whiteboards, tablets, and laptops interchangeably. They are practicing using the best tool for the task at hand, and they are choosing wisely. Seeing these students empowered with choice, the ability to self-regulate, and the skills to pursue learning is indeed amazing.

Empowering Teachers

Just as our students are growing up in a unique time, so are teachers experiencing the pressure to alter our practice in ways that can swing between invigorating at best or downright discomforting. Most of us grew up in the "analog" days where a computer was something you used sparingly and only for highly specific tasks. The new, digital age presents us with opportunities with which we are unfamiliar. Not many teacher colleges prepared us for a classroom where devices are prevalent.

As the administration began to encourage teachers to incorporate the tablets and laptops into the lessons, there was a mixed reaction from teachers, and rightly so. Some classrooms had devices out next to bookshelves so that students could freely grab one and get to work while other classrooms kept the devices locked away only for special lessons. Seeing this was a fantastic opportunity for us to witness all the ways technology could be used in classrooms. Too much access to devices tended to be counterproductive and too little was wasteful of opportunities.

Through discussions with teachers, we found that they were very keen to use the devices but needed help. It goes without saying that teachers are busy. Really busy. There isn't time for them to set up devices for a lesson, get the necessary software or materials, and then run the lesson by themselves. This is where my role as the technology integrator and instructional coach has been transformative.

During planning sessions, my job is to meet with teachers and listen to the inquiries they are leading in their classrooms. They are full of great ideas, and I help to find solutions for them and then prepare devices or the Makerspace for their lessons. Sometimes I lead lessons when teachers are unfamiliar with the technology being used. In this situation, the teacher becomes the student and gets to learn alongside their class (with the benefit of showing their students that we, as adults, are also learners). Often, lessons are gradually transforming them into a co-teaching model as the teacher becomes more familiar with the technology. The result of this model is that after we have completed a series of lessons, the teacher has a new skill to use in their classroom, and we have formed a deep co-teaching relationship where they have seen me work with their students and feel comfortable having another teacher in their room. Other times, a teacher may already know the technology they want to use. In these instances, I co-teach lessons with the teacher to support them, or I simply prepare for them and then allow them to lead.

None of us are experts in technology. There is too much out there to know and be an "expert" in. However, we all are most likely very knowledgeable at something about technology. Whether it's an app on your phone, Microsoft Word, email, Photoshop, or your beloved Kindle, you probably could teach somebody *something* about technology. That is precisely where we all begin. We found that with our combined teaching staff, we had a lot of expertise that could propel us on our journey.

As part of sharing our expertise, our principal and curriculum coordinator designed *sharing success workshops* that happen twice a semester. During these workshops, teachers can highlight one thing they are doing in their class that is going well. Though it is not mandated that they share a success using technology, many teachers do. It is a great opportunity to share ideas and encourage innovative practices for our classrooms. The outcome has been that teachers are freely discussing technology in the hallways and forming positive partnerships between classes.

Allowing teachers to play to their strengths and share successes has been extremely beneficial. Discussions about technology are positive opportunities where teachers feel empowered, and they carry with them a growth mindset. We have dismantled the old idea of professional development, in which teachers are upskilled in a "one size fits all" environment and some feel defeated when they fail to pick up the skills being taught.

Empowering Administrators

We are a Google for Education school, so we have been training our teachers to use Google tools such as Docs, Slides, and Sheets to plan units and communicate with each other. However, working with teachers, we found that they were still using Microsoft Word, PowerPoint, and Excel and not switching to the Google platform. After some deep thinking, we found that this was partially because the administrators were finding it difficult making the same transition. As a result, the documents that were going out to the whole staff were still in Microsoft Word and other Microsoft products. Once we helped the administration transition shared school documents to the Google platform, we found that everyone began to use Google. Not only did they begin to use Google, but they began to teach themselves and share techniques during planning meetings. The result was that we stopped spending time on training sessions, got out of the way, and watched the staff embrace a new platform.

We include our administrators as co-learners in teacher trainings and workshops. This allows them to know what technology is being used around the school and also piques their interest in tech. The overall effect of this is deep and multifold. Our administrators teach in classrooms throughout the school on a rotating basis. They do this so that they keep in touch with the students and also to provide teachers with much-needed planning time. Because of this, our administrators need to know how to use technology in a variety of classrooms. It has been great for them to be successful with tech in classrooms and to share those successes with teachers. It has also given them great insight into the needs of the school when it comes to tech. As a result, our administrators have been highly involved in the development of our technology scope and sequence. They are also able to make insightful decisions when considering budgetary and curricular needs. Lastly, when considering outside presenters for professional development, technology has always been a factor that they want to promote.

Empowering Parents and Building Bridges

The parents and families of our students are major stakeholders on this journey. They certainly deserve the same support that students, teachers, and administrators receive. Our students are living in homes connected with the internet, and most have multiple devices available for use. When the teachers first began to introduce devices into classrooms, many families were uncomfortable with this change and voiced their concerns; but, in the end, they respected our decision. They have been incredible advocates on this journey. We had to ask ourselves, if the parents are supporting us, shouldn't we be supporting them? So we began to build bridges and help our families create safe and healthy digital environments in their homes just as we were creating them at school.

We began by hosting Parent Forums at school to discuss technology. But although the forums received a great initial response from parents, they were often poorly attended. Investigating, we found that we were missing our target of connecting with families in many ways.

First, when the forums were held during the day, any parent with a job or other daytime commitments was unable to attend; and when they were held in the evening, parents had their children at home and found it difficult to leave. Second, we found that a "one size fits all" approach to discussing technology with parents was inappropriate. Just as our teachers carry a variety of tech experiences and skills, so do our parents, and by hosting groups of parents together and not differentiating for them, we weren't supporting our parents the best we could. Lastly, we found that there was a lot of apprehension and nervousness from parents. Many felt poorly equipped to deal with the technological advances around them, especially as they were seeing their children coming home with new technology skills they were unfamiliar with. This made us, as teachers, seem intimidating, and parents were shy to attend our forums, much less speak up at them.

To remedy this, we first wanted to give parents regular, open access to discuss technology with us. We wanted to take away the formal, planned forums and create a community of open, casual discussion and collaboration. We looked at times during the school year when parents are on campus and targeted those days as opportunities.

Nearly every Friday, we have an assembly for the entire elementary school. Many parents attend these assemblies and often come early to beat traffic. Because of this, we created "Techie Brekkie," which is hosted before assemblies during the time that the parents are waiting for the assembly to begin. Techie Brekkie is simple. We began by putting out coffee, tea, and light snacks for the parents. We kept handouts about technology or tablets nearby for them to peruse. I was always nearby. I took the time to get to know the parents, talking with them one on one or in small groups, usually in casual conversation. These casual conversations were the beginning of bridge-building. By getting to know each other, having some laughs and forming relationships, we began to better understand the needs of the parents and how to best support them.

The technology discussions often began about the provocations we set out: information packets, tablets, laptops, robots, and even circuits and carpentry tools. These provocations allowed parents to view and digest as much as they could and then ask more when they had questions. Our more extroverted or confident parents were great at breaking down barriers, asking great questions and working with others for solutions. This empowered others who may not have been so assertive to join in or to seek me out later with their queries.

After one year, Techie Brekkie provided great benefits to the parents and the school. Empowering the parents with a voice in what they want to learn or discuss has been revolutionary. Because of this, attendance for Techie Brekkie has improved because parents know that they help control the topics covered. Our parents have also started bringing their home devices to these gatherings so that I can help them learn how to use and administer them. The parents are also swapping ideas for apps and sharing strategies on how to build a healthy balance with technology at home. The benefit has been that our parents are running safer and better-equipped devices in their homes as well as forging bonds with each other.

Innovative Leadership Practices

Incorporating technology into our classrooms is a challenge that requires flexibility and support from the entire school community. From our journey, there have been some key lessons that have guided our path. First, technology is engrained into our lives. We should look at mirroring that experience for our students so that they can develop healthy lifestyles with technology. Second, our students are our best resources when it comes to learning about technology. They are willing to try new things, learn new skills, and share with others. Third, teachers can all be empowered to incorporate technology into their environments if we switch from a deficit model of professional development to a model that builds on the strengths that teachers already possess. Fourth, administrators are often overlooked when it comes to professional development in technology. They should always be included so they can support purposeful change and foster environments for innovation. Fifth, the home environment for our students is also technology-rich. We should not accept that our students have a dichotomy of experiences with technology between home and school. We should be working with parents to build a consistent experience for our students with technology that encourages the creation of products and growth of skills. With these lessons in mind, we hope that we can develop a holistic program that is inclusive of all members of our community, that fosters digital citizenship in all of us, and that encourages lifelong learning through technology.

Hit the Ground Running: Leveraging Distance Education for Teacher Induction

Jeff Dungan

> **Summary**
>
> Preparing teachers to be successful in their first weeks at a new international school is a phenomenon which all international school leaders grapple with. This chapter highlights one East Asian international school's attempt to front-load new teacher induction by hosting a fully online, asynchronous, self-paced online learning course. The course consisted of five modules, each developing the understanding of various technology platforms that are widely used across all divisions. Teacher feedback and perceptions of the online course and learning experience were collected and informed the school's instructional technology team's further development of the course.

A common conundrum in international schools is how best to prepare teachers for a successful start in a new school and life in a foreign country. Most, if not all international schools, invest significant resources, both financially and human, in ensuring that hired teachers can transition to their new reality as seamlessly as possible. With the many strategies schools utilize to make transitioning from one school and life to another, many new hire teachers struggle in their first months to acclimatize to the culture, practices, and pace of the school. Nowhere is this truer than in large, top-tier international schools.

One aspect of acclimatizing new-hire teachers is to learn the multitude of technology operations and platforms that are unique to the international school. While many schools utilize similar platforms (e.g., student information systems, learning management systems (LMS), printing, computer and tablet operating systems, and hardware), every school is unique. It is not uncommon for a teacher transferring, for example, from a large international school in Beijing, to have to relearn different systems in their new school in Shanghai. It is a case of "same same, but very different."

In many cases, a school's various technology platforms are the interfaces that need immediate attention as they allow teachers to perform basic tasks that are necessary on the days leading to the first days with students. This might include making copies, taking attendance in a student information system, collecting parent contact information to make email distribution lists, creating online content and learning experiences within a learning management system, or simply communicating with other staff and staying abreast of divisional and school announcements via a school's internal communication platform. In addition, teachers normally need to access grade-level or department files and other online resources that are normally housed in cloud-based productivity suites. In short, preparing teachers for the first days is a daunting task, if only considering the instructional technology requirements in order to be productive.

In the spring of 2018, the Shanghai American School (SAS) instructional technology coaches (ITC), in partnership with the director of instructional technology and Shanghai American School's human resources department, embarked on an ambitious goal of creating an online course that would prepare teachers to hit the ground running. This was an effort to empower newly hired teachers to navigate various instructional technology platforms and systems so that they could be productive and successful from the start.

New-hire teachers were surveyed using a tool designed by our instructional coaches to gain insight into their perceptions of the course content, design, and online learning. Valuable insights into teachers' previous experiences with distance education and self-paced learning were also collected to inform the SAS instructional coaching team in making improvements and refinements to improve future iterations of the course.

Course Design

The New Hire Tech Bootcamp Course was designed to be hosted in Schoology. Schoology, like many learning management systems, allows for instructors to build modules of content that can then be published to students. Schoology was chosen in hosting the course because it has the ability to track user analytics, communicate with participants directly throughout the course, post course updates, and host threaded asynchronous online discussions. The discussions were used in this course as a platform for participants to ask questions about the course content and platforms and provide a space for the instructional technology coaches to reply to those. In so doing, early rapport was established between the technology coaches and the incoming new hire teachers.

The decision of what content to include in the New Hire Tech Bootcamp Course was made by the K–12 instructional technology team. This team consisted of five instructional coaches (three from the SAS Pudong campus and two from the SAS Puxi campus) and the SAS director of technology. The course design and content were decided on during a one-day retreat on the Puxi campus. The New Hire Tech Bootcamp Course originally consisted of four modules. These modules covered the four major tech platforms at the school that were used across all three divisions (e.g., elementary, middle, and high school). SAS employs other platforms such as Naviance, a counseling student information system used in the high school. However, since it is only used in one division, the decision was made not to include single-division platforms in the course design.

The four modules that were designed covered Office 365, Schoology, the printing and copying system, and Mac basics for those new hires who were not familiar with the Mac ecosystem. Of these modules, the Office 365 module and the Schoology module were the most robust. This made sense, as Office 365 is the school's online, cloud-based productivity suite. Teachers interface with this platform daily for email communications, to access their cloud-stored documents, to access their working groups where files are shared privately between group members, for calendaring, and to access Microsoft OneNote. Schoology is also another widely used, cross-divisional platform. Therefore, it was important that new hires have exposure to the multiple ways that Schoology is used within the SAS community.

Beyond hosting course content for students, Schoology functions as the attendance-record-keeping site for the elementary school, middle school, and high school staff, and as the grade book for middle school and high school teachers, and it hosts teacher course resources from year to year. In addition, Schoology is SAS's formal communication portal for school–home communications. All upcoming divisional dates, gatherings, and academic calendars are hosted in Schoology, providing parents a single point of contact for all school-related and academic information for their child regardless of whether they have children who span multiple school divisions. The contents of the four modules within the New Hire Tech Bootcamp Course are listed in Table 22.1.

While all four modules were important, when placed together in the course they became a solid foundational piece for new hire teachers in

Table 22.1 Module descriptions

Module	Number of Lessons	Topics Covered in Module
Office 365	6	• Logging into Office 365 and getting started • Using Outlook mail • Using Outlook calendar • Working in Office 365 groups • OneNote basics • Using OneDrive cloud storage
Schoology	9	• Understanding the difference between courses, groups, and resources • Personalizing the Schoology experience by modifying account settings and notifications • Adding course content including understanding folder structures to facilitate student learning and file management • Posting course and parent updates • Taking attendance and entering grades in the online grade book
Printing and Copying	5	• Sending prints to the printer • Logging into the printer • Collecting prints at the printer • Making copies and scan
Mac Basics	5	• Customizing your trackpad, desktop, dock, and hot corners • Locking your screen • Creating folders and subfolders • Emptying trash • Switching sound outputs and language settings

the fall of 2018. The New Hire Tech Bootcamp Course facilitated early points of contact between new-hire teachers and the instructional technology coaches before the first reporting day. Furthermore, the instructional technology team was able to examine New Hire Tech Bootcamp Course analytics and track the progress of participants.

Choosing a Launch Date

International school's human resources departments usually front-load new-hire teacher information starting in the spring of the academic year before the teachers arrive at the school. This front-loading often includes information regarding visa procurement, shipping of personal effects, any necessary medical or work-related records required by the host country, and information regarding new-hire housing options. Following the human resources lead, the Shanghai American School instructional technology coaching team took advantage of front-loading essential information to launch its online New Hire Tech Bootcamp Course. In consideration of the information the teachers were receiving from human resources in the spring, and in an effort not to cause anxiety as departure dates drew near, the team decided that launching their course in late June would provide ample time for the new teachers to explore the topics.

Teachers were emailed detailed instructions on the rationale behind the course, the choice of timing for launching during the summer months, and details on how to log in and access the course through Schoology. Analytics collected from the course indicated that all but two teachers had logged in at least once during the summer months before the July 31, 2018 reporting date for new hires. This data reinforced the assumption the Shanghai American School ITC team had made about the eagerness of new-hire teachers to access job-related onboarding resources during their transitionary summer holiday.

Course Evaluation Findings

In order to judge the effectiveness of the course, both an online survey and face-to-face interviews were conducted with new-hire teachers who were willing to participate and offer feedback. Eighteen new-hire teachers' responses were collected in total. The questions on the survey mirrored questions asked in the online survey so that regardless of the mode of media collection, the data could be compiled and analyzed. Questions were focused on having new-hire teachers reflect on their learning experience within the course, perceptions of online learning, perceptions of the course content and design, and the timing of the course launch over the summer months. Space to offer suggestions for improving the course in future iterations was also included. The course evaluation survey focused on four domains: participants' previous online learning experiences, the relevance of the course content, the overall design and navigation of course materials, and participants' perceptions of online learning.

Previous Online Learning Experiences

From the data collected, we concluded that the online learning experience was an appropriate method to deliver the training content. New-hire teachers were comfortable learning online; all but one had participated previously in online learning. All 18 teachers indicated that self-paced learning suited their learning style and provided flexibility in accessing the learning material. The data also suggested that other professional learning opportunities in international schools might be delivered online as self-paced asynchronous courses. Online learning was an efficient way to deliver such content and it freed the teacher from receiving instruction in a one-time, catch-what-you-can setting that most new-hire teacher induction sessions resemble in the first days of school orientation.

Course Content

All but one of the new-hire respondents indicated they felt the course content was highly relevant to their job responsibilities. This indicated that the course content was applicable and relevant to new-hire teachers. Only two respondents said that the course was not highly applicable to their job responsibilities. One potential reason for this could be that these individuals were not classroom teachers and therefore did not need to know how to navigate the platforms that were covered by the course modules. However, this is also a reminder that differentiating course content on the basis of new-hire roles is an important aspect of new-hire onboarding and training. If participants do not find the material to be pertinent to their school roles, they will be less likely to engage with it.

One consistent theme from the course feedback was that new hires would have liked the modules to be contextualized within the responsibilities of their jobs and the school organization. For example, one new-hire teacher mentioned that she would have liked to see an existing course or two that was already built in Schoology so that she could have "seen it in action." A suggestion was also made to have a short video by one of the instructional technology coaches at the beginning to inform people of the uses of the platform and where they would encounter it organizationally, its function(s), and why it would be important to them. Seeing as this theme emerged across nearly half of the respondents, future iterations of the New Hire Tech Bootcamp Course will include a "Setting the Stage" introduction to each module so that learners have some connection to the material and see where it fits organizationally for them in performing their organizational roles.

Finally, respondents mentioned that course content should be differentiated by divisional needs. Some of the new-hire teachers felt that specific platforms used in specific divisions were missed and that they would have liked to learn more about these prior to their arrival. Two examples of this were from a high school teacher who was unfamiliar with Naviance and then learned about how it was used and its purpose after arriving. Similarly, an elementary teacher noted the omission of Seesaw, an online portfolio and parent communication platform used exclusively in the elementary grades. These findings contradicted the instructional technology team's initial design considerations only to include platforms that were used across all three divisions regardless of staff roles.

Course Design

All but one new-hire teacher indicated that they agreed the course design was easy to follow and the lesson sequencing within the modules was scaffolded toward more advanced skills and concepts. The design of the course was purposely built with consistency and colors to aid in both the course navigation and the consistency in content. New-hire teachers specifically mentioned the consistent theme, color scheme, and folder structure used on all of the lesson pages as conducive to an organized course structure that was easy to navigate.

One interesting finding was that not all respondents liked the use of video in the modules. Twenty-one percent of new-hire teachers surveyed indicated that they preferred learning through text rather than through video tutorials. This was unexpected and suggests that adult learners, unlike millennials, may prefer text or a combination of both text and multimedia for knowledge acquisition. One respondent offered this summation of this notion saying,

> Some things are better than others for being learned online. If I see a video and I have text, the video covers most of what I need. But if there's something with a lot of steps, I might miss it so it's helpful to have the text to go back to—having both is better rather than one or the other.

Another respondent noted that "a print out with each topic with the guidelines or main information, would be helpful—combine a cheat sheet with key points of the platform."

Perceptions of Online Learning

There was a high degree of learner satisfaction with the fact that all the course material was made available at the start of the course. New-hire teachers mentioned that they appreciated being able to "float" between modules and pick and choose the topics that interested them or that they knew little about. Without having sequential, stepwise progression through the course material, learners mentioned that the pace and the presentation of the material were relaxed and easy to digest. The fact that all material was accessible from the start and was available throughout the year meant that new-hire teachers also had a knowledge and self-help repository that they could reference from anywhere at any time when in need of tech support.

Conclusion

Many layers come into play when transitioning to a new school, culture, and life. Familiarizing oneself with a new school, school practices, and new living arrangements and acclimatizing to a new culture and country can overwhelm even the most seasoned and well-traveled of international educators. It was the aim of the instructional technology team to reduce anxiety levels of new-hire teachers by giving them a learning platform to begin the transition process to the school-wide technology platforms well in advance of arrival. This chapter detailed Shanghai American School's attempt at streamlining and expediting new-hire teacher induction using distance education.

The high degree of teacher experience with distance education, learning management systems, and asynchronous learning make distance education highly accessible for new-hire international teachers. In future refinements in the course design and content, we will continue to improve new-hire learning experiences to strengthen and expedite the onboarding of new hire teachers. If schools can minimize even a single aspect of this by using distance education to familiarize new-hire teachers with one important aspect of the school (e.g., technology platforms), it can significantly lower new hires' anxiety upon arrival and expedite the process of getting comfortable and to a place of productivity in their new roles and hit the ground running.

Innovative Leadership Practices

This chapter illustrates an example of how distributive leadership in schools can be leveraged to encourage and develop innovative practices. However, distributive leadership can prove challenging in schools where mid-level leaders and teachers have not received proper training in functioning with purpose, autonomy, and the skills necessary to facilitate groups and group work. School leaders interested in truly empowering their coaches and teacher leaders need to consider investing in their professional learning as well, so that they can handle ambiguity and work collaboratively and productively within groups. Shanghai American School has invested heavily in developing a culture of improvement and reflective practice. This includes sending all instructional coaches to Cognitive Coaching© and Adaptive Schools©, two programs that develop one's ability to coach and lead individuals and groups through protocols and processes to maximize their potential.

Without high-functioning teacher leaders and mid-level leadership, the distributed leadership model in schools risks falling flat. Furthermore, without a culture that empowers and supports teacher leaders and coaches to function with a high degree of autonomy, mid-level leaders often get discouraged with a sense of powerlessness and lack of voice in organizational decision making. Therefore, as illustrated here, school administrators can serve as a support, rather than a driver, for teacher leader groups and coaches, to develop innovative professional learning experiences.

Index

Note: Page numbers in **bold** indicate tables; those in *italics* indicate figures.

absorption system, petroleum 101
academic quality 104
academic success 104, 112
action plan, for inclusion 28–32; *see also* inclusion
adaptive schools 89, 208
adequate professional development 68
advisory structures 146–149
agency 152; inclusive learning 28–29, 30, 31, 32, 33; relational 82–83; student 1–2, 116; teacher 116, 152
agentic learning 31, 152
Al Khawarizmi 45
alumni, database 103
American School Bombay (ASB) 88, 92–93; *see also* cognitive coaching
approaches to learning (ATL) 7, 183
Armstrong, Thomas 29
art and technology 187
ASB *see* American School Bombay (ASB)
assessment: criterion-based 14; goals of 63–64; international mindedness **40**, *41*; performance 77; self 6, 7–8; skill-based 61–70; standards-based 62
ATL *see* Approaches to Learning (ATL)
audit of inclusive learning 26–28, **27**; *see also* inclusion
authentic collaboration 89–90; *see also* collaboration

backward design approach 66
The BAIS Buzz 52
Banjul American International School (BAIS) 48, 49
Being Female in Science (Jarreau) 49
benefits: cognitive coaching 92–93; full-time instructional coaches 89–90; Tech Mentors 91
Beninghof, Anne 155
biannual educational conference 106
BIE *see* Buck Institute for Education (BIE)
blogs 102, 155
BondClegg, Taryn 152
Bonner Curriculum: True Color Personality Styles (workshop) 154–155
bowl setting, classrooms *181*, 182
Bryk, A. 124–125
Buck Institute for Education (BIE) 101, 103–104

Index

Caobos *see* Gimnasio Los Caobos, Bogotá, Colombia
challenges 98–100; in campus life 106–107; cognitive coaching 92–93; developmental 101; equity 164–171; full-time instructional coaches 89–90; leadership 137; provocations and 20; teacher leaders 140; Tech Mentors 91
change, FLoW21 114–115
change management strategies, Caobos 102–107; innovative and traditional practices 104–105; intentional communication 102–103; local and global partnerships 105–106; student voice 106–107; transformational professional development 103–104
changes: to classroom practice 45–46; to curriculum 44–45; international mindedness 43–46; in teacher recruitment 43–44
children with special rights 82
choice workshops 30, 155
circular learning model 185, *186*
classrooms: in the bowl setting *181*, 182; cloud 14–15; flipped 184–185; guide on the side setting 182, *182*; inclusive 30; individuals 13; paradigm shift 117; partnerships 105; as research hubs 183; roundtable conferencing *181*, 182; sage on the stage setting 180, *180*; settings 180, *180–182*, 182; smarter 180–182, *180–182*; societies (humanities) 13; technology-integrated 185; walls 158; without teachers 13–15; *see also* physical learning spaces; technology
CLE *see* community learning exchange (CLE)
cloud classrooms 14–15

coach/coaching *see* instructional coach/coaching
co-constructed and personally relevant curriculum 114
cognitive coaching 92–93
cognitive learning space 186–187
cohort structure 127
collaboration: authentic 89–90; group norms of 147, *147*; hub 184; interactive project focused approach 183; peer interaction and 186; skills 102
collaborative leadership 56
collaborative problem solving 20
collective efficacy 63
communication skills 124
communities, as learning space 188–189
community learning exchange (CLE) 125–130, **128**, 165
community learning group 117
competencies 100–101, 105–106, 119, 120
competency-based curriculum 119, 120
competency-based progression 114
connected learning community 1:1 laptop program 162
connections 154–155
constructivist theory 154
Convention on the Rights of the Child 111
conversation-mapping hack 140–142, *141*
COP-24 *see* Council of Parties (COP-24) in Poland
co-practitioner researchers (CPR) 164, 165–166
copying and printing 202, **203**
Council of Parties (COP-24) in Poland 100
course(s): content 205–206; design 202–204, **203**, 206–207; evaluation 204–205; *see also* iBlock courses

Index

course sequence 128–129
CPR *see* co-practitioner researchers (CPR)
creativity 19–21
criterion-based assessments 14
Csikszentmihalyi, M. 115
Cuban, Larry 115
culture: defined 155–156; of safety 68
culture of learning 150–159; in action 157; building 155–157; innovative leadership practices 158–159; lifelong learning 158; making connections 154–155; overview 150–151; purpose 151–154
curriculum 71–79; competency-based 119, 120; components 73; connecting parents to 168–169; freedom within structure 73–74; internationally minded 38, **39**, 41, 44–45; macro 73, 74–79; mapped 77; micro 75–76; overview 59–60; responding to societal changes 72–73; standards 74; unit-level 73

Damon, William 100
Dar es Salaam International Academy, Tanzania, Africa 177–179
database 103
de-privatization of learning 158
design facilitator 89–90
design for learning 156
design thinking 95; authentic collaboration 89–90; play environment 16–18
design thinking in pedagogy 177–189; community 188–189; in digital learning spaces 184–188; innovative learning spaces 186–188; in physical learning spaces 179–184
developmental challenges 101
developmental disabilities 106
Dewey, John 104

Diago, Felipe 100–101
Diago, Gabriel 101
didactic learning 129
digital learning spaces 178, 184–188; circular learning model 185, *186*; flipped classrooms 184–185; fostering inclusion 185; peer interaction and collaboration 186; visible thinking tools 185; *see also* physical learning spaces
digital literacy coach (DLC) 90–91, 94; *see also* tech mentors
Diploma Programme (DP) 4, 41
disabilities 106
dissertation 129–130
distance education, for teacher induction 200–209; course content 205–206; course design 202–204, **203**, 206–207; course evaluation findings 204–205; module descriptions **203**; online learning 205, 207; overview 200–201; selection of launch date 204
distributed leadership: advisory structures 146–149; in teacher leadership 137–138
DLC *see* Digital Literacy Coach (DLC)
doctoral program *see* reimagined doctoral program
Down Syndrome 101
dramatic play 14
drone 102
Dweck, Carol 152

EAL *see* English as an Additional Language (EAL)
early childhood (ages 2.5 to 6) 26
Early Years School (EYS), at Nido de Aguilas 16–18
East Carolina University International Ed.D. 123–126, **128**; community

learning exchange (CLE) 125–130, **128**; improvement science 124–130, **128**
edcamp 155
Edmondson, Amy 155
EdTech Facilitator 89
education 111; factory model of 152; see also distance education, for teacher induction
educational blog 102
educational change 106
educational ecosystem 111
Ekomuro 107
ELL see English language learning (ELL)
English as an Additional Language (EAL) 89–90, 157, 166
English language learning (ELL) 170
Enhanced Primary Years Programme (PYP) 152
entrepreneurship projects, Caobos 101–102
environmental impact 107
equity challenges 164–171; innovative leadership practices 171–172; participatory action research (PAR) 165–166, 168–169
essential agreements 193
expert 7
explicitly reinforcing skills 183–184
exploration courses 5; description of 6, **6**; goal setting 6, 8; self-assessment 6, 7–8; see also iBlock courses
extrinsic motivation **151**

Facebook 187
factory model of education 152
faculty community forum 148
faculty & staff learning group (WAB) 117
Fisher, Darlene 162
flexicard scheme 189
flipped classrooms 184–185

FLoW21, WAB 111–115; 21 targets 112–114
fostering inclusion 185
Freire, P. 104, 129
Friend, Marilyn 155
full-time instructional coaches 88–90; benefits and challenges 89–90; staffing structures 88–89
future of learning at WAB see FLoW21, WAB

Gimnasio Los Caobos, Bogotá, Colombia 98–108; blog 102; challenges 98–100; change management strategies 102–107; globally connected learning 100–102; innovative and traditional practices 104–105; intentional communication 102–103; local and global partnerships 105–106; overview 98–99; project-based learning (PBL) 100–102; purpose-driven student-centered learning 100–102; social media presence 102–103; student voice 106–107; transformative professional development 103–104
Gladwell, Malcolm 152
globally connected learning 100–102
goals 72–73; assessment 63–64; iBlock 10; independent 74; innovative 99; learning 74, 75–78; longer-term 10, 74; long-range 80; primary instructional 63; project 56; short-term 5; trans-disciplinary 75
Gomez, L. 124–125
Gonzales, David Felipe 107
Google 196
Google Doc 82
Google Drive platform 14, 32
Google Office Suite 14

Index

Grunow, A. 124–125
guide on the side setting, classrooms 182, *182*

hacks 140–142
Halligan, Kristin 168–171
Hayden, Mary 162
Haythem, Ibn 45
Heath, Chip 153
Heath, Dan 153, 155
hydrocarbons 101

IB *see* International Baccalaureate (IB)
iBlock courses 3; change process 9; concerns/challenges 8–9; explorations 5, 6, **6**, 7–9; interdisciplinary 5, 6, **7**; leadership decisions and lessons 9–11
IEP *see* Individual Educational Plan (IEP)
Ignotofsky, Rachael 51
improvement science 124–130, **128**
inclusion 25–33; action plan 28–32; audit 26–28, **27**; in digital learning spaces 185; inquiry and learning 29–31; systems and structures 31–32; vision for 28–29
inclusive learning 26, 28–33; agency and 28–29, 30, 31, 32, 33; partnership 28, 29; strength-based 28, 29–30; *see also* learning
individual education plan (IEP) 14, 30
individualized schedules 114
Individual Learning Plan (ILP) 14
innovation fair 101
innovative and traditional practices 104–105
innovative leadership 93; advocates 94–95
innovative learning spaces 177–189; art and technology 187; cognitive space 186–187; digital space 178, 184–188; physical spaces 178, 179–184; turning space into visible thinking tools 187
in-person learning 129
inquiry, student-led 104
inquiry-based research 77
instructional coach/coaching 82, 87–96; advocates 94–95; American School of Bombay 92–93; cognitive 92–93; collaboration in 93–94; digital literacy 90–91; full-time 88–90; International School of Beijing 88–90; leadership 95–96; long-term change 95; overview 87–88; success factors 93–96; United World College Southeast Asia 90–91
instructional leadership 29–30, 68
instructional technology coaches (ITC) 201
integration: of art into technology 187; of technology into art 187
intentional communication 102–103
interactive collaboration project focused approach 183
intercultural skills 100
interdisciplinary courses 5, 6, **7**
International Baccalaureate (IB) 29, 38, 43, 152, 162, 179, 183
International Baccalaureate Diploma Program 72
International Baccalaureate Primary Years Programme (IB PYP) 168
International Baccalaureate's New Enhanced PYP (IBO 2018) 30
International Baccalaureate World School 3
International Day of Women and Girls in Science 49–50
international mindedness 37–47, **39–40**; assessment **40**, 41; changes

Index

43–46; curriculum 38, **39**, 41; diverse school community 38; multilingualism 38; pedagogy **39**, 41; practices **39**, 45–46; survey 38; teachers **40**, 41–43

International Partnership for Climate Change in Canada 100

International School Bangkok (ISB) 29, 71–79; *see also* curriculum

international school community 68

international school leaders 123, 133

International School Nido de Aguilas, Santiago, Chile, 135–137

International School of Beijing 88–90; *see also* full-time instructional coaches

International School of Uganda (ISU): creativity at 19–21; culture of learning 151–154; inclusion at 25–33; technology in 191–192

interviews 51

intrinsic motivation **151**, 152, 157

Intrinsic Motivation Week 186

ISB *see* International School Bangkok (ISB)

ISU *see* International School of Uganda (ISU)

ITC *see* instructional technology coaches (ITC)

Killoran, Tosca 165–166, 170

King, Martin Luther 100

Kohn, Alfie 152

Kotter, John 9

KWL process 169

lab-based investigations 76

lab-based skills 77

Lǎoshī 165–166

leaders: international school 123, 133; teachers 135–144; *see also* school leaders

leadership 95–96; advocates 94–95; challenges 9, 63, 66, 137; collaborative 56; distributed 137–138, 146–149; hacks 140–142; instructional 29–30, 68; lessons learned 9–11; role 21; students systems 106–107

leadership decisions 1, 9–11; act on vision 10; communicating vision 10; consolidate learning 10–11; creating and sharing the vision 10; need 9–10; planning short-term win 10; sense of urgency 9–10; set longer-term goals 10–11; strategic focus 10

leadership role 21

Leading Change: Why Transformation Efforts Fail (Kotter) 9

learning 29–31, 81–83; agency 28–29, 30, 31, 32, 33; agentic 31, 152; circular model 185, *186*; in cloud 14–15; cognitive space 186–187; communities 117–118; culture 150–159; de-privatization of 158; design for 156; distance education 200–207; inclusive 26, 28–33; in-person 129; leading own 13–14; lifelong 158; online 129, 205, 207; partnership 28, 29, 30, 31; self-directed 113–114, 152; strength-based 28, 29–30, 32; *see also* inclusive learning; professional inquiry

learning communities, WAB 117–118

learning diversity 29

learning spaces: communities as 188–189; digital 178, 184–188; innovative 177–189; physical 178, 179–184; WAB 118

learning support assistants (LSA) 27

learning support services 26

learning systems & structures group (WAB) 117

LeMahieu, P. 124–125

Index

lessons learned *see* leadership decisions
LGBTQ+ students 107
lifelong learning 158
local and global partnerships 105–106
long-term change process 95
lower elementary (ages 6 to 8) 26; school librarian 89
LSA *see* learning support assistants (LSA)

Mac basics 202, **203**
MacDonald, James 162
macro curriculum framework 74–79; components 74–75; development and use 74–79; mapping 77–79; micro curriculum and 75–76; performance assessment tasks 77–78; PK-12 subject team meetings 76–77
Madonna, Erin 166
making connections 154–155
Malaguzzi, Loris 32
mapping a plan forward 139–140
McTighe, Jay 72–73
Medical Research Council Unit The Gambia at the London School of Hygiene & Tropical Medicine (MRCG at LSHTM) 49–56
meetings, team 143
micro curriculum 75–76
middle path 104–105
Middle Years Programme (MYP) 4, 5, 6, 41
Mi Mundo, Mi Pasión/My World, My Passion senior capstone project 106
Ministry of Education, Colombia 105
Mission Street (video game) 101
module 202–204, **203**
motivation 55, 69, **151**, 151–152, 157; *see also* extrinsic motivation; intrinsic motivation
MS/HS Design Facilitator 89

MS/HS EdTech Facilitator 89
multilingualism 38
Murdoch, Kath 152
MYP *see* Middle Years Programme (MYP)

networked improvement communities (NIC) 125
Neurodiversity in the Classroom (Armstrong) 29
New Hire Tech Bootcamp Course 202–207, **203**
New International School of Thailand 29
Next Frontier Inclusion (NFI) 26
Next Generation Science Standards (NGSS) 66
novice 7

Office 365 202, **203**
oil spills 101
one-stop shop 32
online learning 129, 205, 207
Opening Doors and Closing the Gender Gap 49

Padlet 185
PAR *see* participatory action research (PAR)
paradigm shift 117
parent forums 197
parents: connecting to curriculum 168–169; database 103; engagement in education 102–103, 108; technology and 197–198
participatory action research (PAR) 165–166, 168–170, 171
partnership 32; BAIS 49; co-teaching 30; learning 28, 29, 30, 31
PD *see* professional development (PD)
pedagogy: design thinking in 177–189; international mindedness **39**, 41; separate 33

216

Index

peer interaction and collaboration 186
performance assessment tasks 77
personal learning journeys (PLJ) 21, 31, 150–151, **151**, 152, 155–156, 158; see also culture of learning
personal learning profile (PLP) 32, 81–83
petroleum absorption system 101
physical disabilities 106
physical learning spaces 178, 179–184; classrooms as research hubs 183; explicitly reinforcing skills 183–184; interactive collaboration project focused approach 183; smarter classroom 180–182, *180–182*; see also digital learning spaces
pitching process 13–14
PK–12 subject team 76–77
plastic chemical land mines in Colombia 102
playground 16–18; brainstorming 17; challenges on 17; committee 16–17; creative 17; design/redesign 17–18; problem statement 17
PLJ see personal learning journeys (PLJ)
PLN see professional learning network (PLN)
PLP see Personal Learning Profile (PLP)
political climate in Colombia 99
Powell, Christie 166–168, 170
practitioner 7
Prain, V. 83
Primary Years Programme (PYP) 4, 41, 152, 153
printing and copying 202, **203**
professional development (PD) 68, 103–104, 150–151, **151**; see also personal learning journeys (PLJ)
professional inquiry 29–31; capacity for all staff 29; capacity for leadership 29; inclusion 25–33; see also learning

professional learning network (PLN) 29
program, reimagined Ed.D. 127–130; cohort structure 127; course sequence 128–129; dissertation 129–130; in-person learning 129; length 127; online learning 129
program length, reimagined Ed.D. 127
progression, competency-based 114
progressive education 99
progress mentor program, WAB 119
project-based learning (PBL), Caobos 100–102

quality see academic quality

Reggio Emilia study 82
reimagined doctoral program 122–131, 164–172; cohort structure 127; community learning exchange (CLE) 125–130, **128**, 165; co-practitioner researchers 130; course sequence 128–129; dissertation 129–130; East Carolina University International Ed.D. 123–126; features 127–130; Halligan, Kristin 168–169, 170–171; improvement science 124–130, **128**; innovative leadership practices 130–131; in-person learning 129; Killoran, Tosca 165–166, 170; Lăoshī 165–166; length 127; online learning 129; overview 122–123; Powell, Christie 166–168, 170; principles 124
Renault 101
research, women in science 50
research and development labs 30
Revolución Educativa (educational blog) 102
Revolution in Education Congress 106
Rodriguez, Sara 107
roundtable conferencing, classrooms *181*, 182

sage on the stage setting, classrooms 180, *180*
Saldarriaga, Nicolás 106
Santamaria, Sofia 107
SAS *see* Shanghai American School (SAS)
schedules and timetables, WAB 118–119
Schooling by Design (SbD) (Wiggins and McTighe) 72–73
school leaders 117, 136, 155, 208; creating a school culture 150; distributed leadership 149; international 123, 133; role 155; teacher leaders 138, 161
School of 600 Teachers (database) 103
Schoology 202–203, **203**, 204
schools, creativity in 19–21
science: improvement 124–130, **128**; women in 48–57
scientist reflections 54–55
self-assessment 6, 7–8
self-directed learning 113–114, 152
self-management 99, 104
seminars 139–142
senior educational leadership team (SELT) 111–112, 114–116
settings, classroom 180, *180–182*, 182
Shanghai American School (SAS) 201–204
shared leadership *see* distributed leadership
sharing success workshops 195–196
Shiffman, Dan 162
Simpson, Caroline 48
Sinek, Simon 153–154
"sit and get" education 99
skill-based exams/assessment 61–70; assessing targeted skills 66–67; goals of 63–64; identifying problem 62–63; planning instruction 65–66; prioritizing standards 64–65; shifting to 67–70; unique features of 62
skills 8, 11, 20, 100, 183–184; areas 7; based exams 59, 61–70; building 6; collaboration 102; communication 124; development 2, 3, 5, 30, 65, 156; explicitly reinforcing 183–184; intercultural 100; lab-based 77; learning goals 77; media literacy 50; targeted 66–67; teachers' 103; transfer 64
smarter classroom 180–182, *180–182*
social constructivist theory 154
socially supportive learning environments 21
social media 102–103, 155
space, pedagogy, and conceptual knowledge (SPACK) 178–179, *179*
special rights 82
staffing structures: cognitive coaching 92–93; full-time instructional coaches 88–90; technology mentors 91
stakeholders, WAB 112–114
standards-based assessment 62
STEAM labs 89
steering committee, WAB 116
structures: advisory 146–149; cohort 127
student(s): advisory forum 146–147, *147*; cloud classroom and 14–15; collaboration skills 102; empowerment 192–194; exchange programs 105–106; holistic development 119; leadership systems 106–107; leading their learning 13–14; pitching process 13–14; products 101–102; voice 106–107
student learning group, WAB 117

Index

student-led inquiry 104
student reflections 53–54
Switch: How to Change Things when Change is Hard (Heath and Heath) 153

takeaways 55
targets 112–114
teacher(s): agency 116, 152; classrooms without 13–15; distance education 200–207; international mindedness **40**, 41–42; technology and 194–196; turnover 100; *see also* distance education, for teacher induction
teacher leaders/leadership 135–144; conditions for 138; distributed leadership 137–138; innovative leadership practices 143–144; leadership hacks 140–142; lessons learned 142; mapping a plan forward 139–140; overview 135–137; seminars 139–142; team meetings 143; theory of action 140
team meetings 143
tech board 94
Techie Brekkie 198
tech mentors 90–91
technology 191–199; administrators and 196; art and 187; overview 191–192; parents and 197–198; students and 192–194; teachers and 194–196
technology mentors *see* Tech Mentors
technology solution, WAB 119–120
tertiary education 111
theory of action 140
three beliefs 28–31, 33
timetables and schedules, WAB 118–119

Tooher-Hancock, Oli 162
tools, visible thinking 185
Towards Inclusion: Planning Our Path: An Inclusive Audit Protocol 26
Toyoda, Sakichi 153
TPACK framework 178
traditional exams 62, 64, 65, 67
transfer skills 64
transformation plan, WAB 115–120; competency-based curriculum 120; learning communities 117–118; learning spaces 118; progress mentor program 119; schedules and timetables 118–119; steering committee 116; technology solution 119–120
transformative professional development, Caobos 103–104
True Colors: Exploring Personal & Leadership Style (workshop) 154–155
Twain, Mark 153
21 targets 112–114

unconference 155
Understanding by Design (UbD) (Wiggins and McTighe) 72
United Nations International School, Hanoi 3–4; *see also iBlock* courses
United Nations Strategic Development Goals 9
United World College Southeast Asia (UWCSEA) 88, 90–91; *see also* Tech Mentors
Universidad de la Sabana in Colombia 101
upper elementary (ages 8 to 11) 26

"Vasudhaiva Kutumbakam" 46
video game 101

visible thinking tools 185, 187
vision: acting on 10; communicating 10; creating and sharing 10; for inclusion 28–29
visiting scholars program 161–163
Von Frank, V. 136

wall, provocation 19–20
Western Academy of Beijing (WAB) 110–121; competency-based curriculum 120; educational ecosystem 111; FLoW21 111–115; foundation 111; innovative leadership practices 121; learning communities 117–118; learning spaces 118; mission 110, 111; progress mentor programs 119; schedules and timetables 118; stakeholders 112–114; technology solution 119–120; transformation plan 115–120; vision statements 111
"We teach as we were taught" 152
Wiggins, Grant 72–73
WiSP *see* Women in Science Project (WiSP)
women in science 48–57; bulletin 51–52; discussion 55–56; interviews 51; luncheon 52; participant experiences 53–55; research 50
Women in Science: 50 Fearless Pioneers Who Changed the World (Ignotofsky) 51
Women in Science Project (WiSP) 49–56
Wylie, M. 41

Yokohama International School (YIS) 161–163
young people 100

For Product Safety Concerns and Information please contact our EU representative GPSR@taylorandfrancis.com
Taylor & Francis Verlag GmbH, Kaufingerstraße 24, 80331 München, Germany

www.ingramcontent.com/pod-product-compliance
Lightning Source LLC
Chambersburg PA
CBHW062215300426
44115CB00012BA/2065